UNIVERSITY FUNDRAISING IN BRITAIN
A TRANSATLANTIC PARTNERSHIP

UNIVERSITY FUNDRAISING IN BRITAIN

A TRANSATLANTIC PARTNERSHIP

WILLIAM SQUIRE

Matador
9 Priory Business Park
Kibworth Beauchamp
Leicestershire LE8 0RX, UK
Tel: (+44) 116 279 2299
Fax: (+44) 116 279 2277
Email: books@troubador.co.uk
Web: www.troubador.co.uk/matador

ISBN 978-1784620-097

The cover photograph of graduating students is reproduced by kind permission of
Jonathan Taylor and Hughes Hall, Cambridge

British Library Cataloguing in Publication Data.
A catalogue record for this book is available from the British Library.

Typeset in Aldine by Troubador Publishing Ltd
Printed and bound in the UK by TJ International, Padstow, Cornwall

Matador is an imprint of Troubador Publishing Ltd

To Sarah

Contents

Foreword

This account of the development of fundraising by British universities is timely and important. It is based on the author's wide practical experience, which ranges from establishing fundraising at Cambridge University to advising educational institutions internationally on how to broaden their sources of income. The history of the development of educational fundraising in Britain deserves an official record in its own right. It also carries lessons for other not-for-profit bodies, which need in times of austerity to solicit support for their activities.

There were a number of obstacles or objections to overcome in order to raise funds for higher education successfully in Britain. First, the post 1945 level of support by taxpayers for universities had by any standards been extremely generous. For students like myself and for the academics who taught us, further education seemed at the time to be a publicly funded good. Ingrained attitudes therefore had to be changed along with the acceptance of tuition fees. Both constituencies, those who benefited from higher education and those whose calling was teaching and research in institutions of higher education, had to look outwards and learn to persuade potential funders of the importance and worth of their cause.

There were more general inhibitions about asking for money that needed to be overcome, primarily on the academic side. The case for raising money for higher education was in order to broaden access to its benefits and to sustain the intellectual reputations of the institutions concerned. Their reputations in turn depended on the quality of the academics who staffed and led them. Academics therefore had to be fully involved in fundraising and in meeting with prospective donors. They needed to see it not as a diversion from their academic work but crucial to its continuance. Cambridge, as a collegiate university, also had to address the issue of bringing together the fundraising of the colleges with that of the university. This was achieved with the 800th Anniversary appeal.

This book documents the culture change involved and the new attitude to fundraising it engendered, which is now seen as an integral part of university leadership. This change was the work of many hands. It required the active support of lay leaders outside the academic world and a readiness to learn from best practice in North America. The author writes from first hand knowledge and experience of building relationships with alumni and of recruiting and training those entering the new career of professional fundraising. I witnessed these developments as a member of the Jarrett Committee on university management and through my involvement with fundraising at Cambridge and Aston Universities.

What this book also chronicles is the emergence of the new profession of fundraising. Fundraising for long term sources of income, which was what educational institutions required, involved establishing development departments which could provide the necessary functional support. While the leadership had to come from within the institution, American experience demonstrated the need to recruit skilled and dedicated support teams to turn their fundraising strategies into effective action. For the institutions involved this meant an initial investment in staffing in the expectation of a future return. It was thanks to the example of the US educational sector that this act of faith could be justified. The author gives full weight to the debt which those who developed funding for higher education in Britain owe to the co-operation and generosity of their American counterparts.

The fundraising profession in Britain is an essential adjunct to achieving the financial goals on which the survival of a wide variety of not-for-profit activities depend. Its role in education helped to lead the way and it is now accepted as providing the discipline and professionalism for successful fundraising across the board. There is still a lack of senior staff with the necessary experience in the organisation of effective fundraising. A further contribution which the educational sector can make is to ensure that members of their development departments have a valued career path ahead of them.

William Squire's book will be of interest to a wide readership. The lessons from the development of university fundraising are relevant beyond educational boundaries. They apply wherever there is a need to attract funds for all manner of charitable or cultural activities. They have implications for government in framing their policies on taxation. The social and financial importance of encouraging these sources of revenue deserves the study of politicians and those in the public service. They will find useful guidance in this book.

Educational fundraising is still work in progress. Understanding how it began and first developed will help to shape its future. It is a matter of great satisfaction that an activity, once seen as unnecessary, and even 'below the salt', has proved its worth in a wide range of universities and colleges throughout the country. Long may it continue and flourish.

Adrian Cadbury

Introduction

Britain has a long and creditable history of voluntary giving to charitable causes – Poppy Day, the Lifeboats, the RSPCA, Cancer UK, Oxfam and many others have become household names with millions of regular supporters. Education has, in the modern period, not attracted the same degree of charitable support, though the great civic universities of the nineteenth century owed their existence to local philanthropists backed by local subscription. In the United States the philanthropy which funded early colleges like Yale, Princeton and Harvard was supplemented in the nineteenth century by the growth of publicly funded colleges and universities, endowed initially through federal land grants to every state.

In recent times Britain and other European countries shared with the United States a common ideal of what a university should be. This was unashamedly elitist and based on the Prussian model of the early nineteenth century; it embodied the concept of a community of scholars and students engaged in learning, teaching and research, and free as individuals to pursue truth within an autonomous institution governing its own affairs. The model was funded differently in different countries. In the United States, and the UK until World War I, the top universities were largely privately funded, whereas in continental Europe universities were the responsibility of the state.[1]

The transition to mass higher education in the twentieth century put an increasing strain on all sources of funding. In the United States, with its active tradition of philanthropy, this led to an early emphasis on fundraising across the sector, the historic example of the private universities being quickly followed by state-funded institutions. In continental Europe, state funding continued to dominate.

---

[1] See 'The Ideal of a University Today', Professor Robert Anderson, March 2010, at www.historyandpolicy.org.

In the UK, between the World Wars, funding was divided roughly 50/50 between public and private sources. With the growth of the welfare state this 'mixed' funding soon gave way to a model almost totally dependent on the state. A whole generation of students and academics grew up seeing higher education as a free entitlement. In the 1980s, university leaders, conscious of the need to maintain international standards, were increasingly aware of the limitations of state aid to meet the growing need for updating teaching and research facilities. Some began to consider fundraising as a way of mobilising significant resources to supplement state provision.

By 1983 a dozen universities had completed one-off appeals raising sums ranging from a few thousand pounds to £2.1 million. By the end of that decade both Oxford and Cambridge had announced campaigns of over £200 million each, a different order of magnitude. At the start of the new millennium more than twenty universities had invested in fundraising programmes. Politicians of all parties were increasingly aware of the limitations of the current 'free' model for the financing of the expanding British university system. Government initiatives under New Labour led to an explosion in university fundraising, so that by 2012 some 160 higher education institutions had active and continuing programmes.

This account traces the achievements of a handful of academics and an early generation of fundraisers in bringing about remarkable cultural change. Adapting North American best practice to local circumstances, this group of people pioneered a new role for philanthropy and a greater professionalisation of fundraising in British universities.

PART I

The National Picture

1
UK context

Background

The ancient universities in England and Scotland were the beneficiaries of financial support from monarchs and bishops from earliest times. The service of Commemoration of Benefactors held annually at Cambridge lists names going back to Eleanor of Castile in the 13th century. Until World War II, British universities still derived roughly 50 per cent of their revenue from private sources. The expansion of higher education in the post 1945 period led to a sea change whereby universities and students alike became largely dependent on the tax payer. This policy of expansion was supported by all political parties on grounds of social justice and utility, recognising the importance of a properly educated population for the success of a modern economy.

As a result, successive generations of British students from 1945 benefited from the most generous system of student support in the western world. Depending on parental income, many enjoyed a free university education. Foreign students also benefited from this system until differential fees for home and foreign students were introduced in a controversial measure in 1980-81.

By 1971 student numbers, at almost 500,000, were more than double the post war figure; they doubled again in the next twenty years to 1.2 million.[1] This unprecedented expansion meant that the academic world had 'little respite from the job of simply coping with rising numbers'.[2] Yet the Government remained

---

[1]   *The Times*. 'Cry from the Ivory Tower'. 24 February 1992.
[2]   Department of Education and Science (DES). (1972) *Education: a Framework for Expansion*. Cmnd. 5174, London: HMSO, para 4.

committed to funding further expansion, though concerned 'to arrest the tendency for unit costs (per student) to rise'.[3]

Just as students had come to take for granted that the tax payer would fund the costs of a university education, including living costs, successive generations of academics had been conditioned to expect the state to meet the needs of the higher education system as defined by the universities themselves. They now had increasingly to justify their activities by reference to external criteria. As a matter of government policy universities were expected 'to contribute more effectively to the improvement and performance of the economy'.[4]

Yet government exhortations to universities to develop outside sources of funding fell largely on deaf ears at the institutional level. As late as the 1980s the academic consensus was that it was the duty of the government to provide the funds universities required; and that to seek supplementary sources of funding from private sources was wrong and would be 'letting the government off the hook'.

There was further fear that acceptance of funds from outside sources could lead to conflicts of interest which might jeopardise academic freedom at the individual level, and at the institutional level risk damaging a university's reputation. These fears arose primarily in the research field when collaboration with, or acceptance of support from, commercial sponsors might restrict freedom to publish, or even to the distortion of research results.

These concerns were less prominent where philanthropic gifts were concerned. Many universities had benefited from support from the great philanthropic foundations in the UK and the US even before World War II (for instance the Carnegie and Mellon Foundations' support for university libraries). Nevertheless, there was a nascent concern that individual benefactors would seek to influence the use of their gift to the detriment of academic freedom.

Such concerns, reinforced by the cost implications and the uncertainties of

---

[3]   Ibid., para 129
[4]   DES. (1985) The Development of Higher Education into the 1990s. Cmnd. 9524, London: HMSO, para 1.2.

success in initiating a new policy of active fundraising, must have given pause to the leaders of UK universities. They were thus cautious in exploring the possibilities for institutional fundraising from external sources, though ad hoc arrangements for research cooperation with industrial partners was widespread. In this period UK universities, whilst willing to receive, were not yet ready to ask.

The insistence on government funding was based on the assumption that the arms' length arrangements would continue, whereby funding reached universities via the University Grants Committee, itself imbued with the prevailing university ethos, rather than direct from a government department. This buffer function was continued in a weaker form through the higher education funding councils which replaced the UGC following the Education Reform Act of 1988. More importantly government funding reflected the prevailing view of universities as autonomous bodies comprising independent-minded academics unhampered in their quest for intellectual truth.

This concept was reaffirmed in the Magna Charta Universitatum signed by rectors of European universities in September 1988 which included in its list of fundamental principles 'which must now and always support the vocation of universities' that: 'The university is an autonomous institution… its research and teaching must be morally and politically free of all political authority and economic power'.[5] The declaration was notably silent on the sources of funding which would enable these principles to continue to be put into practice.

By the end of the 1980s in Britain the ups and downs of the economic cycle and competing claims on the public purse led the Thatcher government to press universities to control costs and diversify their sources of revenue. This step required a revolution in attitudes and a change of culture within the academic community. The cuts of the early 1980s led to substantial loss of funding for the sector and gave a major jolt to conventional thinking. Until that time, the reliance on the state as the main source of funding for both recurrent and capital

---

5   Observatory Magna Charta. (1988) *The Magna Charta Universitatum.* [online] http://www.magna-charta.org/.

expenditure had the negative effect of funnelling the intercourse between academic leaders and the world outside academe into one main channel – a dialogue with the government. There was little incentive for the academic world to communicate with its other key constituencies – its alumni, the general public from which its students come, and the world of work to which its graduates go. Although there were many individual contacts between academics and leaders in all walks of life – the business world, media and the arts, the law and other professions – there were few universities in the post war period which saw any need to institutionalise and build such relationships as a way of developing financial support for the work of a university.

However, by the 1980s it was clear that universities would have to diversify their sources of income, or be faced with a deterioration in the quality of teaching and research, coupled with the implicit danger that the leading British universities would fail to maintain the best international standards.

Many British academics were familiar with the higher education system in the United States, and recognised that the top American universities, whether private or state in origin, were among the best in the world in terms of intellectual achievement, while also serving utilitarian ends and promoting social mobility. When the time came to pursue an active fundraising policy, the US example was to prove an important source of best practice.

Post war expansion

From the end of World War II there was a steady increase in the number of young people in higher education measured by absolute numbers and as a proportion of the relevant age groups. This policy of expansion was based on both idealistic and utilitarian considerations, with politicians and academics laying differing stress on differing aspects at different times.

This development originated in the 1944 Education Act[6], presented to parliament by R.A. Butler, the (Conservative) Minister of Education in Churchill's wartime government. This 'great education act [...] inaugurated momentous changes in the

---

[6]   Education Act 1944 (7 and 8 Geo. 6 c.31) London: HMSO.

organisation of education in the schools'.[7] In enabling the expansion of provision for secondary education, it gave local authorities in Britain the power to give scholarships and allowances so children could stay at school beyond the minimum leaving age (fifteen) in order to qualify for university entrance. It also empowered local authorities to give similar financial support to school leavers qualifying for university entrance. By increasing the supply of school leavers qualified for university entrance the Act initiated a national policy of university expansion which by the early 1960s had more than doubled the pre war number of students:

1938–39	69,000
1954–55	122,000
1962–63	216,000 [8]

In 1961 Sir Edward Boyle, then Secretary of State for Education in the Conservative government of Harold Macmillan, commissioned the landmark report on higher education by a commission chaired by Lord Robbins which paved the way for some new universities and a further major expansion in student numbers. The much quoted axiom on which Robbins based his recommendations was that 'courses of higher education should be available for all those who are qualified by ability and attainment to pursue them, and who wish to do so'.[9] This idea was based on the twin arguments of benefit to the nation and benefit to the individual: 'We do not believe modern societies can achieve their aims of economic growth and higher cultural standards without making the most of the talents of their citizens' and 'education ministers intimately to ultimate ends in developing man's capacity to understand, to contemplate and to create'.[10] It was further argued that the British economy was falling behind its international competitors because of the lack of educated manpower in the modern age. The comparison with the US was particularly striking. According to the Robbins Report (1963) the UK had at that time thirty-three students per 10,000 population whilst the US had 125.[11]

---

7   Committee on Higher Education. (1963) Higher Education: Report of the Committee Appointment by the Prime Minister under the Chairmanship of Lord Robbins 1961-63). Cmnd. 2154, London: HMSO. (Robbins Report).
8   Robbins Report, op. cit., Table 3, Chapter III, p15.
9   Robbins Report, op. cit., p8, para 31.
10 Robbins Report, op. cit., Chapter II, paras 32-3.
11 Robbins Report, op. cit., para 122-3.

Robbins recommended the doubling of the student population; ten years later in 1971 the student population had more than doubled to 463,000 and was predicted to expand further to an estimated 750,000 over the next decade. The proportion of the age cohort entering higher education was rising substantially:

1961   actual 7%
1971   actual 15%
1981   estimate 22%[12]

The Robbins Report took for granted that the cost of this expansion would fall on the tax payer, and balanced this cost increase against the national interest argument for a better educated population. Noting that, historically, British universities had been independent of the state, Robbins pointed out that the position had changed: 'all depend on large grants from the state to enable them to carry out their present functions'.[13] The Report noted that 'in North America income from private sources provides a greater share of income of institutions than in Britain'.[14] But Robbins failed to see the possibilities for multiple sources of income other than the state alone, and there was thus no serious discussion in the Report of the possibility of developing other revenue streams for universities. A pale reflection of the possibility of fundraising did appear in the conclusion, where vice-chancellors were recommended to 'keep in touch with potential benefactors'[15] – hardly a trumpet call to action. The result was the most generous system of student support from public funds in the western world – a policy which for decades was non-controversial and received all-party backing.

Links with industry

The Labour government elected in 1964 was as keen on university expansion as its predecessors. But it placed renewed emphasis on the contribution British universities could make to the economy. Harold Wilson had made a famous

---

12 DES. Cmnd. 5174 op. cit.
13 Robbins Report, para 15.
14 Robbins Report, para 128, p.45.
15 Robbins Report, op. cit., para 676, p.121.

speech at the Labour Party Conference in Scarborough in 1963, the year before becoming prime minister, on the implications of scientific and technological change and 'the Britain that is going to be forged in the white heat of this revolution'. Thus the government in particular urged universities to expand their links with industry aiming for technology transfer in the form of new commercially viable technologies, thus increasing the payback from the nation's investment in the universities' basic research.

One well-placed observer of the relationship between industry and university research departments was Stephen Bragg, an engineering graduate of Cambridge and MIT, who had spent over twenty years in industry. In the 1960s he was chief scientist at Rolls Royce, responsible for liaison with universities. His comment on university attitudes to industry at this time was that pressure for contacts came almost entirely from the side of industry: 'Universities in the 1960s were little interested in cooperation with industry. The universities didn't wake up till the seventies, and the real transformation came in the eighties and nineties when universities began to feel their duty to open up to the wider community'.[16]

In Cambridge a committee was set up under Sir Neville Mott, the Cavendish Professor of Experimental Physics (and a Nobel prize winner), to consider how best to respond to the government initiative. The Mott Committee's report in 1969 made a number of recommendations, notably one that urged an 'expansion of science-based industry' close to Cambridge to take maximum advantage of the concentration of scientific expertise, laboratories and libraries in the university, and to increase the interaction between industry and the Cambridge scientific community. It took a little longer for the change of culture in engineering and science departments to spread to the higher education community at large.

One result of the Mott Report was the decision by Trinity College Cambridge to seek planning permission to develop a science park on land on the outskirts

---

[16]   Stephen Bragg, Rolls Royce 1951-71, (Chief Scientist 1960-63, Chief Research Engineer 1964-68); Vice-Chancellor Brunel University 1971-81; later Administrator American Friends of Cambridge University. Conversation with author, 16 December, 2011.

of the city which had been owned by the college since the reign of Henry VIII. A planning application was made in the autumn of 1971 and the first company moved in in 1973. A number of universities were thinking on similar lines (Heriot Watt opened its science park on the Riccarton site outside Edinburgh in 1974) and, though science parks were often slow to take off, they are now a regular feature of the university scene.

These early efforts to encourage universities to cooperate more closely with industry were not aimed at relieving financial pressures on universities, but on maximising economic returns from university research. Nevertheless, the good relations with industry established by university departments on the basis of contract research grants paid dividends later when universities learned to use their relationships with the corporate world to generate broader financial support.

The evolution of government policy

Meanwhile, so long as successive governments were publicly committed to funding the growing number of students, universities had little need or incentive to diversity their sources of revenue. Indeed the mechanism chosen by the government to channel funds to universities had the unintended consequence of inhibiting a university from developing private sources of revenue. The University Grants Committee (UGC) was set up by the Chancellor of the Exchequer in 1919 'to inquire into the financial needs of University Education in the United Kingdom, and to advise the government as to the application of any grants made by Parliament towards meeting them'.[17]

This initial advisory role grew to cover administrative responsibility for the allocation of grants to universities, and involvement in planning university development. After World War II the UGC was given additional responsibility for the expansion of the university system. The UGC, however, operated what was in effect a system of deficiency payments. Universities estimated their own revenue and expenditure over a five-year period and, once the estimates had

---

[17] The National Archives. *Records of the University Grants Committee.* [online] http://discovery.nationalarchives.gov.uk/SearchUI/Details?uri=C1300.

been agreed with the UGC, the shortfall between revenue and expenditure was made up by a grant from the UGC, adjusted as necessary over a five-year cycle. Thus, if a university reduced its shortfall by an increase in revenue, the grants receivable from the UGC were reduced.

The growth of the higher education sector meant that by the 1980s such an open ended system of financing was no longer acceptable as a proper means for the control of public expenditure. The UGC was replaced by the Universities Funding Council, set up by the Educational Reform Act of 1988, which in turn developed into separate funding bodies for England, Scotland, Wales and Northern Ireland (to take account of the devolution of power over higher education to regional bodies). A recent management statement for HEFCE (Higher Education Funding Council for England) gives its purpose as to 'promote and fund high quality, cost effective teaching and research meeting the diverse needs of students, the economy and society'. [18]

The inevitable critics of the policy of university expansion were roughly grouped into two classes. There were those who thought expansion had gone far enough, or indeed too far, so that 'more meant worse'; and that the universities were not using their resources efficiently, and were failing to turn out the right sort of graduate. And those who thought it was the state that was driving down standards by treating higher education like a production line and failing to fund it properly. Regardless of all arguments, the expansion in student numbers (including of course the growth in women and of post graduate students) continued, even though the size of the eighteen- to nineteen-year-old cohort was expected to fall by 33 per cent in the period 1984-96.

At the same time government pressures were increasing on the universities to make better use of their resources. In 1984 the universities themselves commissioned a report, 'Efficiency Studies in Universities'.[19] This report made recommendations to the government on such issues as longer term funding of universities and a review of the basis for allocating funds; and to the universities

---

[18] Higher Education Funding Council for England. Management Statement between DfES and HEFCE, June 2006. [online] http://www.hefce.ac.uk/.

[19] CVCP. (1985) Report of the Steering Committee for Efficiency Studies in Universities. London: CVCP (Jarratt Report).

on how to improve their governance and management. The government, while continuing to press the universities for greater efficiency, made the Robbins axiom for the provision of higher education even more liberal by changing the criteria for eligibility from 'those qualified by ability and attainment' to 'all who can benefit'.[20] At the same time severe financial restrictions were imposed by Conservative governments in the 1980s. In the five years to 1984-5 there was a reduction in spending in real terms of 3.5 per cent.[21] The White Paper on the development of higher education into the 1990s, already cited, explained that 'continuing gains in efficiency'[22] would be needed until 1987-88.

There is little doubt that in the 1980s academic morale suffered from the efforts made by university administrations to achieve the 'efficiency gains' which cuts in recurrent funding imposed. Academic tenure was limited and restrictions were placed on existing tenured posts, which universities were given the power to terminate on grounds of redundancy or financial exigency. Universities often resorted to deferred maintenance to help balance the books which meant that academic buildings were deteriorating. 'Substantial and quite rapid cuts'[23] in capital spending had also been imposed by the government as early as 1980-81.

In response to the financial squeeze, a growing proportion of universities were now exploring, some more actively than others, how to diversify their sources of income. Increasingly universities were seeking support from business and the great charities; some were establishing science parks to develop commercial applications from research into commercially viable companies.[24] Others set up 'industrial units' to assist science departments to establish links with industry and to advise academics on procedures for patenting and licensing their ideas. One or two were even considering (rather gingerly) fundraising from their alumni and others.

This effort to mobilise private support for teaching and research was encouraged by the government. The 1985 White Paper urged the universities to be

---

[20]   Cmnd 9524 op. cit., para 3.2.
[21]   Ibid., para 9.1.
[22]   Ibid., para 9.3.
[23]   Ibid., para 8.5.
[24]   The first science park in England was established in Cambridge by Trinity College in 1973.

concerned with attitudes to the world outside higher education; it repeated earlier government urgings for universities to develop links with industry and commerce and improve their local connections. To encourage universities to develop greater financial independence the government gave the important assurance that 'increases in income from outside sources will not lead to reductions in government funding',[25] thus removing a major disincentive for universities and potential donors alike.

This White Paper also made explicit reference to the need to broaden the basis of university funding beyond the tax payer, and, given the wider constraints on public finance, emphasised 'the importance to higher education of seeking to derive more of its income from sources other than the tax payer and rate payer ... more income and support can be obtained from business and private sources ... the government wishes to encourage and support the necessary effort'.[26]

It took almost another twenty years for HMG to back up these admirable sentiments with financial inducements to universities to start up a fundraising operation, and to encourage them to persevere through a matching grant scheme for funds raised.

University authorities in the United States, which saw a similar if not greater expansion in student numbers in the post 1945 generation, took a different course in tackling their financial problems. A comparison with the position reached there is instructive.

---

[25] Cmnd 9524 op. cit., para 1.9.
[26] Cmnd 9524 op. cit., para 9.4.

2:
The US context

Background[1]

The history of higher education in the United States is marked by the growth of 'every kind of trade, vocational and career institution as well as college and university programmes'. This diversity has resulted in a hierarchy of institutions with modern research universities at the top. Already by the time of the Revolutionary War, the American colonies had nine chartered colleges[2] compared with just two[3] – Oxford and Cambridge – in England. To these largely private foundations were added an increasing number of state institutions to meet the growing needs of an expanding economy. This push for state support of higher education was most notably embodied in the Morrill Land Grant Act of 1862. This Act gave every state resources for the endowment and support of 'a college of agriculture and mechanical arts', and has been described as 'the most important piece of educational legislation ever passed [in the USA]'.[4]

Philanthropists who were instrumental in the development of the private universities also played an important part in the growth of the land grant

---

[1] This and the following section draws in part on the *article History of American Higher Education: Pursuing the College Degree*. Random History. (2008) [online] http://www.randomhistory.com/1-50/039degree.html.

[2] They were: Harvard, William and Mary, Yale, Philadelphia, Princeton, Kings College (Columbia), College of Rhode Island (Brown), Queens College (Rutgers) and Dartmouth.

[3] Or three if the Inns of Court are counted. Scotland had four (Aberdeen, Edinburgh, Glasgow and St Andrew's).

[4] Morison, S and Commager, H (1950) *The Growth of the American Republic, Vol II*. New York: OUP, p.310.

colleges. A case in point is Cornell, where Ezra Cornell's benefactions, combined with federal grants under the Morrill Act, enabled the new university to open in 1868.

Post World War II expansion

The decades after World War II marked the next great expansion of higher education in the United States. Whilst college attendance grew between 1920 and 1930 from 53,000 to 140,000[5], the great expansion after World War II was based in large part on the Servicemen's Adjustment Act (GI Bill), 1944. Some 4.4 million World War II veterans went to college out of 15 million veterans benefiting from various provisions of the GI Bill.[6] 'Between 1950 and 1990 the number of colleges and universities almost doubled from 1851 to 3535.'[7]

The wide variety of institutions involved – public, private and commercial – meant that developments in the financing of higher education took a very different course from the UK. The great expansion in student numbers strained private and public institutions alike. The GI Bill meant there was a substantial injection of public funds throughout the system, whether the institution was private or public. The private institutions which had a tradition of philanthropic support, and had developed a tradition of professional fundraising, intensified their efforts, particularly from alumni. The state universities and colleges, mainly reliant on state and local taxes and who tried to keep tuition fees low, discovered that, because of the vagaries of the economic cycle. they could not always rely on state legislatures to fund or maintain their expanded programmes. They too therefore turned increasingly to fundraising.

Thus public and private institutions alike needed to seek additional resources

---

5 National Centre for Education Statistics (NCES) Digest of Education Statistics, Washington DC, Dept of Education.

6 Archibald, Robert B. (2002)*Redesigning the Financial Aid System: Why colleges and universities should switch roles with the Federal Government* Baltimore MD: The John Hopkins University Press.

7 Lazerson, M. '*The Disappointments of Success : American Higher Education after World War II*': Annals of the American Academy of Political Sciences, Vol 559 (September 1998) quoted in *History of American Higher Education* op. cit.

to sustain this democratisation of higher education. Together with the growth in population, this led to a massive increase in the number of students enrolled in higher education and in the proportion of the US population over twenty-five who had completed college.

Table 1[8]

	1945	1975	1993
US Population (million)	140	215.5	259
Number of students (million) enrolled in higher education	1.677	11.185	14.385

Table 2[9]

Percentage of US population over 25 years old who have completed college

1940	1945	1955	1965	1975	1985	1995	2005
4.9	5.1	7.0	9	14	19	23	27

The demand created by such an expansion was met by a wide variety of institutions – two and four year state-funded colleges, private colleges, 'research' universities, 'for profit' educational institutions, and colleges run by major companies to meet their own educational needs.

State colleges and universities, by now having learnt the vagaries of tax support as it bent to the economic climate, began to follow the private institutions into serious fundraising. For their part, private institutions developed public sources of support in the form of federal grants , particularly for research.

_____

[8]   Adapted from Tables 4.1 and 4.2. Cohen, A, Kisker, C. (2010) *The Shaping of American Higher Education*. Jossey-Bass: A Wiley imprint. John Wiley + Sons, Inc.
[9]   Adapted from figure 3.1. Bowen, W, Kurzweil, M., Tobin, E. (2005*) Equity and Excellence in American Higher Education*. Charlottesville and London: University of Virginia Press.

Percentage of revenue by source for public and private institutions 2004-05 [10]

	Public Institution %	Private Institution %
Tuition and Fees	16	30
Federal, State and Local government	49	15
Endowment Income and Gifts and Grants	7	34
Other	28	21

The 7% of revenue of public institutions derived from endowment income and gifts and grants, cited above, broke down as follows:

	1993-94 $	2004-05 $
Endowment Income	639 million	10.4 billion
Gifts and Grants	4.5 billion	7.8 billion

Private institutions were attracting even more support proportionally than the figures for public institutions quoted above. But the growth in philanthropic income of publicly funded institutions over the decade 1994-2004 is striking; the support generated showed that, in the USA, public as well as Ivy League institutions could run successful fundraising programmes.

The growth of philanthropic fundraising in the United States in support of education (including schools) can be further illustrated as follows:

---

[10] Adapted from Table 6.9. Cohen, A., Kisker, C. op.cit. p. 535.

Charitable Giving to Education for selected years 1945-2010 [11]
$ billion

1945-6	1955	1965	1975	1985	1995	2000	2010[12]
0.161	0.571	1.5	2.16	7.5	12.75	22.5	28

It will be noted that by the mid 1980s, when the British government began to urge UK universities to consider raising private funds for higher education, donors in the United States were already giving $7.5 billion a year in support of education. The growth of fundraising on such a scale necessitates a degree of specialisation, professional training and investment by the institutions concerned which was several orders of magnitude greater than any activity in UK universities.

Early in the post war period it was clear to American educators that a new administrative area involving the external relations of an institution had emerged, in which fundraising was an important component. By the 1950s in all types of higher education it was taken for granted that the relationship of an institution with its alumni, its friends, the local community and the public authorities needed careful and professional management, including fundraising, in which the head of the institution had to be personally involved. The discussion in the US was not about *whether* the president of a university should be involved, but how best to organise and support his or her's involvement and what sort of professional was needed to provide that support.

The Greenbrier Conference and the formation of the Council for Advancement and Support of Education (CASE)[13]

This massive growth in fundraising required some major organisational changes

[11] See relevant editions of "Giving USA" 1960, 1965, 1976, 1986, 1996, 2001. [online] http://www.givingusareports.org/.

[12] 'Voluntary Support of Education 2010', p.2 (Council for Aid to Education). [online] http://cae.org/fundraising-in-education.

[13] CASE is a not for profit organisation of institutions and professionals involved in fundraising, alumni relations and PR in universities, colleges and schools, based in Washington DC.

within universities and a concomitant investment in specialised staff and related activities. The expansion in American higher education and the variety of institutions in which it was carried out led to the ad hoc growth of non academic programmes to mobilise public support for this expansion. Post World War II the functions of public relations, alumni relations and fundraising existed in some form on most campuses, but there was a growing awareness of the need for organisational and administrative coordination. Although there was no one ideal organisational pattern, there were some common principles on which each institution could make its own decisions.

In 1958 the American Alumni Council (AAC) and the American College Public Relations Association (ACPRA) held a joint study group to consider these issues. The conference was supported by the Ford Foundation and held at The Greenbrier in White Sulphur Springs, West Virginia. The organisers took the view that the strength and quality of US higher education depended to a large extent 'on the degree to which the public understands and is willing to support our colleges and universities'[14]; and that it was thus urgent to develop effective programmes to advance public understanding and support. While this was obviously true of public institutions heavily dependent on the state legislators and the taxpayer, it was equally true of private institutions, whose prime constituency was their alumni body and other friends and supporters. Yet there were no established guidelines or patterns of organisation to inform such institutional development.

The conference was preceded by a wide consultation exercise where a variety of college and university presidents, as well as AAC/ACPRA members, were consulted by questionnaire on the organisational issues for the handling of fundraising, alumni relations, governmental relations and public relations as follows:

---

[14]   Foreword to the Report and Conference. Joint ACPRA-AAC (American Alumni Committee) Study Committee. (1958) *The Advancement of Understanding and Support of Higher Education: a Conference on Organizational Principles and Patterns of College and University Relations.* Washington DC: American College Public Relations Association (The Greenbriar Report I).

Institutions Reporting	Questionnaires returned by AAC/ACPRA Members	Questionnaires returned by Presidents
Tax supported	65	131
Private	69	104
Church supported	33	40
Independent church related	54	110
	221	385

This table[15] is cited to show the degree to which university presidents were already in the 1950s being engaged in these organisational issues, including the role they should play in fundraising. The contrast with the position in the UK, where vice-chancellors only began to be seriously involved in fundraising some thirty years later, is striking (see chapter 5 below).

There was also clear recognition of the need to upgrade qualifications of the personnel engaged on these non-academic tasks. Unsurprisingly the call was made to increase the budget for these activities.[16] The conference thus dealt principally with the internal mechanisms needed for a college/university effectively to cultivate important external constituencies, invariably including alumni, the general public at local or national level, central and local government, and the corporate world, especially in the institution's own geographical area. All these themes were to be addressed at the policy level in the UK some fifty years later in the Thomas Report and the Pearce Review (see Chapter 7 below).

The other main objective was to consider the various means of lightening the university presidents' day to day burdens of engagement with these broad areas of government, public relations, internal communications and fundraising.

This is not the place to follow in detail the consequences of the Greenbrier programme. Suffice it to say that university and college leadership alike eventually saw the logic of the analysis. Even so, it took another twenty years (1974) for the two professional organisations concerned – the American College

---

[15] Table taken from P.76, Appendix III of Greenbrier Report I op. cit.

[16] Foreword to the Greenbrier Report I op.cit. (item 7).

Public Relations Association (ACPRA) and the American Alumni Council (AAC) – to achieve a successful merger and to form an integrated organisation: the Council for Advancement and Support of Education (CASE). Its aims and objectives included 'to continue and further develop sound relationships between educational institutions and their supporting constituencies ... and to offer programmes that develop professional skills in publications, fundraising, public relations and management'.[17]

One of the great strengths of CASE was, and is, its use of the volunteer principle. This applied to its governing body of trustees, elected by the institutional membership, and at all regional and sub regional levels. Similarly the national and regional conventions and training programmes were, with the help of the small professional staff at CASE HQ in Washington DC, entirely staffed and run by CASE volunteers. Thus, whatever the topic, the speakers and presenters were all volunteers drawn from the professionals employed by universities and colleges and who carried the responsibility for the activities they were discussing. In addition, CASE was always open to for-profit companies and those who provided services and technologies necessary for the whole spectrum of fundraising, alumni relations, IT support and PR activities.

For those involved in 'development' work at whatever level, they found in CASE a simple mechanism for getting in touch with people like themselves, who were carrying similar responsibilities and facing similar problems. For those coming new to the work it was often with a huge sense of relief that they learned at a CASE workshop or institute that the problems they were facing were not unique to them or to their institution, and that there were ways and techniques for tackling them.

This unselfish dissemination of best practice on a voluntary basis and at all levels of responsibility explains to a great degree the standing of CASE as the leading organisation in its field. Put simply, members found its activities useful and beneficial in improving the professional performance of themselves and their staffs.

The continuing positive view of the role of CASE amongst the professional

---

[17] See www.case.org.

staff directly involved is reflected in the breadth and recent growth of its institutional membership. At the internal merger in 1974 institutional membership (almost entirely North American) stood at 1835. Thirty-five years later in 1989 this had grown to 3204 of which less than 10 per cent was estimated to be from foreign countries. By 2010 global membership stood at 3418 from 74 countries (see also Appendix A).

It is notable that much of the growth in CASE membership in North America is relatively recent. Yet a common perception of UK academics and administrators was that fundraising in US universities was a longstanding activity linked to the great fortunes of the nineteenth century and carried out mostly by private institutions. Thanks to this perception, it was inferred that there was little of relevance to be learned from the experience of CASE members in the US. Yet the way CASE as an organisation developed in response to internal needs indicated the contrary. Staff members in UK universities, charged with the new duties of fundraising and alumni relations, faced similar problems to those in the US, and were struggling to put their limited resources to best use. They naturally turned to the United States to see how far experience there was relevant to UK conditions. This led to a process through which a few individuals in the UK and in the US helped to spread the word which led to major organisational changes.

3

External relations of UK universities – the first steps

Media relations

With the expansion of the student population – and hence in the number of families potentially interested in the universities – and growth in university partnerships with industry and business, it was natural that universities would increasingly seek to communicate with their various constituencies, and in the process remind government of the positive contribution of the higher education sector to the wider public good. In addition, universities, like any other organisation, were learning how to tackle bad publicity, disseminated much more freely in the era of television, as the student unrest in the 1960s had shown.. In some cases this was handled on an ad hoc basis, but by the 1970s a majority of British universities had appointed press and information officers. Usually such appointments were at a low level, being seen as experimental and with an essentially defensive remit from the academics of 'for goodness sake keep the press off our backs'. But gradually the positive concept of getting across to a broader public the contribution of universities to society at large, and the direct benefit of a university to the local and national economy, came increasingly to the fore.

As with any new development, universities acted individually. Oxford and Cambridge, for instance, took opposite routes. Cambridge was one of the last and Oxford was among the first to appoint an information officer. The Oxford appointment was on the basis of a 1965 paper[1] prompted in part by the need

---

[1] 'The role of an Oxford University information Officer', 10.X.1965, W. Kirkman. Copy of an internal memorandum given to the author by Mr. Kirkman.

for press coverage in relation to the Franks Commission on the governance of the University (1966) which in turn arose from the student unrest in the early 1960s. The first appointment was unsuccessful since the postholder was not given the standing or access needed; but within a few years the post and its role were better understood. This development reflected the general position in British universities. Nationally the information function was well established in a majority of universities by the 1970s.

Many of the early appointments were former journalists, so quite early on (in 1967) university information officers formed a professional association for regular meetings and conferences on matters of common professional interest.[2] The polytechnics too had established their own grouping of information officers on similar lines.[3] Having professional journalists in their ranks to set standards, both groups were in good standing with their respective authorities. In addition the national bodies representing respectively universities and polytechnics appointed their own information staff who liaised with their colleagues in higher education institutions.[4]

Alumni relations

The appointment of the first alumni officers followed on naturally from the work of the information officers. There were, in many universities, volunteer-led 'Old Student Associations' or graduate societies, sometimes with minimal secretarial support from the university. In Scotland the older universities were obliged to keep up to date records of their alumni, since all graduates formed part of a 'General Council' with a defined constitutional position. As a result such universities were legally obliged to maintain an up to date electoral register. Some English and Welsh universities had a similar statutory body. But in almost all cases the state of the registers in terms of current graduate addresses left much to be desired.

---

[2]   SCUIO – Standing Conference of University Information Officers.

[3]   PPRISC – Polytechnics Public Relations and Information Services Council.

[4]   Committee of Vice-Chancellors and Principals (CVCP) was the national body representing universities; and the Committee of Directors of Polytechnics (CDP) represented the then polytechnics. With the transformation of polytechnics into universities in 1992 the two bodies merged into Universities UK (UUK).

Once regular communication with the entire alumni body had begun (rather than just with the typically small group of former students mostly living locally) it was natural to contemplate, at least on an experimental basis, an 'appeal' to old students, often for scholarships or some one-off objective. Thus the first steps into organised fundraising were taken.

Boosting university income

In 1984 the Conference of University Administrators (CUA, the national professional body) sponsored a report[5] by a working group of university administrators on ways of supplementing university income. After considering general sources such as overseas student fees, letting university facilities for conferences during vacations, and income from industry and commerce, over half the report – published in booklet form - was devoted to the new areas of alumni relations and fundraising. It included the results of a questionnaire in the spring of 1984 on current practice in the field of alumni relations and fundraising. Thirty-four institutions responded, giving the first outline of the national situation. Of these, twenty-four had a voluntary graduate association of some sort, though the report queried how useful it was to talk about a statutory body with out of date records and little or no staffing or funding to develop alumni programmes. The report compared this with an (ideal) voluntary body with computerised records and back up from the parent institution, and added that it was clear the membership and activity of a number of voluntary graduate bodies were declining because of lack of interest from new graduates.[6] A notable exception was the London School of Economics which had an external relations department for student recruitment, including one part time and two full time members of staff working exclusively on alumni relations, including regular mailings to 34,000 out of the School's 39,000 alumni. Overall the report noted that a substantial number of colleges and universities had not accorded any high priority to alumni relations.

---

[5]   'Conference of University Administrators (CUA). (1984) *Boosting University Income: Report of a CUA working party on supplementary sources of funding for universities in Great Britain*. London: CUA. (CUA Report).

[6]   Ibid. p. 70.

The report came out just before the explosion of information technology consequent on the spread of cheap personal computers. The authors noted this potential tool for improving current clerical records, enabling a mailing system to include selective mailings by geographical area or subject studied. They commented that such databases were already common in the United States, with some sophisticated programming to include family and career and even gift details, 'though it is doubtful that most British university projects would need or want to get to that level'.[7]

On fundraising the report noted some key factors from US experience:

The need for professional staff led by an officer 'at a fairly high level'; 'however valuable the contribution of volunteers [...] a fundraising campaign [...] will need some professional back up.'[8]

The role of the vice-chancellor or principal: 'Any sustained fundraising programme [...] will require the vice-chancellor to develop a very positive role and to have a full commitment to income generation [...] [he]is the main external representative of the institution'.[9] (This point was emphasised by reference to a recent book, *The Power of the Presidency*, by Dr James Fisher, a former university president and at that time President of CASE. Yet it was to take another fifteen years for vice-chancellors to get to grips with what this entailed, and still longer for fundraising to become part of the standard job description for aspirant vice-chancellors).

The scale of resources needed: 'you might do well if associated expenditure is limited to 20% of income'.[10]

The report also had a short section on professional fundraising firms. Again, it was educating its readers from first principles, noting that the issue was not a simple choice between employing a fundraiser to conduct an appeal and not employing one. Consultants could provide a wide range of services and expertise to support a university's policy and support its needs for instance in

---

[7]   Ibid. p. 40.
[8]   Ibid. p.52.
[9]   Ibid. p. 7.
[10]   Ibid. p.55.

recruitment, staff training, drafting marketing plans and fundraising literature and so forth.[11]

This was a prescient comment since universities were slow to see the 'value added' which a good consultant could bring. A common attitude amongst university administrators was to query the concept (as well as the expense) on the grounds that since a (presumably) competent development director had been appointed, why would she/he need further advice? It was not until vice-chancellors themselves became involved in the policy, along with major donors, that the value of constructive external advice and audit of the fundraising policy and operational efficiency became apparent. As a result a number of consulting firms subsequently played a role in developing university fundraising programmes. Some major US firms extended their operations to the UK and later to other European countries, recruiting some experienced UK professionals in the process.[12] A number of university staff, who had begun as administrators or development staff, moved on to the private sector as consultants, to the great advantage of the spread of best practice throughout the UK higher education sector.

It would be facile to criticise the CUA report for the modesty of its aspirations and recommendations. They were far from self evident or accepted practice at the time. From the heart of the educational establishment and with little overt support from vice-chancellors and principals, the group had first to argue the issue of principle: was it right to acquiesce in the government's repeated urgings to universities to diversify their sources of income away from virtual total reliance on the tax payer?

Ray Footman, then Director of Information at the University of Edinburgh, was one of the authors of the CUA report and showed great awareness of the argument that fundraising from private sources could enable the government

---

[11]   Ibid. p.53.
[12]   Examples include, amongst others, John Glier of Grenzebach Glier & Associates, a Chicago-based firm whose European operation was headed by the author after leaving the University of Cambridge, and Brakeley, another US firm headed in Europe by John Kelly, the convenor of the working group which authored the CUA report when he was Bursar of Bedford College, London.

to avoid its responsibilities for funding higher education properly. Writing in the *Times Higher Education Supplement*, Footman commented: 'We certainly do not believe that by so doing [i.e. fundraising from non-governmental sources] we "sell the pass" on the principle of state funding.' [13]

The CUA report booklet's stated purpose was to provide a 'manual of practical information'[14], so it might be thought that a discussion of principle was outside its remit. However, it did raise the issue of principle by quoting the Minister for Higher Education that 'the reality of academic freedom requires them [the universities] to have some resources of their own'[15]. Moreover, in the same *THES* article Ray Footman made clear that 'we shared the view that there was nothing intrinsically wrong with the notion of universities raising more money than they presently do from other than traditional i.e. government sources'.[16]

Thus the assumption was that external fundraising was a worthwhile activity. Given that the great civic universities of the nineteenth and early twentieth centuries including University College London, Leeds, Birmingham, Bristol and Sheffield – the list is a long one – had all been funded by a combination of private philanthropy and public subscription, the basic assumption could hardly have been otherwise. Yet this report from the heart of the educational establishment felt it necessary to argue the point.

It is noteworthy that in a report so sensitive to academic opinion, there was no discussion of the ethics of fundraising and the possible conflicts of interest that could arise between an outside source of funds and academic freedom. The potential for such a conflict of interest was not a live issue at that time. With the growth of fundraising of all kinds, philanthropic and non-philanthropic, the risks were later to become more apparent (see Chapter 6 below).

As it was, the report gave a green light to UK universities from an impeccably orthodox source to explore or expand these new activities, and blessed the

----

[13]   Footman, R. (1984) Earning Power. *Times Higher Education Supplement*. 27 July 1984. p. 12.

[14]   CUA Report op.cit, p. 5.

[15]   Ibid p. 5.

[16]   *THES*, op. cit, 27 July 1984, p. 12.

exploration of the North American experience in fundraising, albeit with many express reservations about differing culture and levels of wealth.

The Edinburgh example

By the early 1990s a number of universities – including Aberdeen (which ran a campaign around its quincentenary in 1985), Bath, Bristol, Durham, LSE, Nottingham, UCL and Warwick, as well as Oxford and Cambridge – had all begun to professionalise their fundraising. The University of Edinburgh has as good a claim as any to have played a significant role in the early stages of the development of fundraising in the higher education sector, so it is worth considering its example in more detail.

Edinburgh had been one of the first universities to appoint an information officer (1971) for general reasons of crisis management. The oil crisis of the early 1970s and the resulting pressure on public expenditure gave added reason for universities to get out a positive message to a wider public about the benefits to society of the higher education sector. Moreover, with the expansion of the sector, more and more families had an interest in 'student' issues, so higher education became more newsworthy. In 1976 Edinburgh University recruited Ray Footman from the Committee of Vice- Chancellors and Principals (CVCP) in London to run a new information office. As was typical for the time, the office was under-resourced for the job, the total staff consisting of himself and a secretary.

In 1982, in preparation for Edinburgh's 400th anniversary celebration in 1983, Ray Footman had paid a six week visit to universities in the US and Canada to see how PR and alumni relations (and, inevitably, fundraising) were handled there. He was therefore well placed to interpret the North American scene to his Edinburgh colleagues and subsequently to a wider group in higher education nationally. The successful organisation of Edinburgh's 400th anniversary celebrations, the programme of events and the outreach to the alumni body, led the then Principal, Sir John Burnett (Principal and Vice-Chancellor 1979-1987), to agree to an expansion of the information office and the addition of an alumni officer in 1984, one of the earliest such full time appointments in the country.

A further noteworthy event (though its full significance was not realised at the time) was Principal Burnett's decision to authorise an appeal for funds in connection with the anniversary celebrations. An appeals officer was appointed (1982). Rather than making this a university post, implying a continuing policy of university fundraising, the post was linked to the General Council (the statutory body of graduates) and to the 400th Anniversary, thereby implying this was a temporary arrangement. Some £43,000 was transferred to the General Council from the university budget to fund this work. This turned out to be the first step in establishing one of the earliest modern fundraising offices in a UK university.

The officer appointed was Iain More who had had relevant experience in the US and Australia. More had studied in the US (University of Oregon) and had gone on to work as a volunteer fundraiser in McGovern's 1972 Presidential Campaign. He had subsequently been involved in successful grant applications for social causes to major US foundations (Ford and Johnson and Johnson). His appointment to Edinburgh gave him first hand experience in fundraising in the environment of a British university.

This small office raised £440,000 by 1983 for Edinburgh University's 400th anniversary which encouraged the university to incorporate it in 1984 into a university development office, still with a small staff of less than half a dozen. In a further significant development, Burnett appointed a group of younger entrepreneurial academics to supervise the new development office, among whom was a young American lecturer in Scottish politics, Henry Drucker, who was later to head the University of Oxford's first fundraising team.

Fundraising in the mid 1980s: the national picture

It is obvious from the low-key way the creation of a fundraising arm was handled that Principal Burnett was well aware of the controversial (among the academic community) nature of what he was doing – controversial because the majority opinion in the academic world was that the government should fully fund the needs of the higher education sector. This attitude was not peculiar to Edinburgh but widely shared throughout the national academic community.

The University of Edinburgh was not alone in taking the first hesitant steps in creating a professional fundraising arm. The CUA report also included (in response to its questionnaire) a list of universities which had completed 'appeals' (sic) in the period 1977-83: the nomenclature is important since an 'appeal' implies a short term activity for specific purposes, rather than an on-going policy of fundraising. Of the twelve universities listed, five had raised between £1 million and £2.1 million; and seven had raised sums between £5,000 and £440,000. They were Aberdeen (£2.1m), Bristol (£100k), City (£9k), Edinburgh (£440k), Hull (£100k), King's College London (£1.5m), Leeds (£375k), Leicester (£21k), LSE (£1.5m), Nottingham (£1.4m), Queen's University Belfast (£1m) and St Andrew's (£470k).[17] The universities concerned were not committed to a permanent fundraising organisation. The examples quoted above were invariably one-off appeals. But the wide geographical spread and number of these universities suggested a growing realisation that British universities were entering a period when additional revenue from non-governmental sources was needed, which in turn would require a more professional approach to fundraising.

Despite the caution and low expectations expressed in this 1984 CUA report, and with fundraising targets calibrated in the thousands rather than the millions of pounds, in less than five years Oxford had launched a £220 million campaign (1988) and Cambridge one for £250 million (1989). From a national point of view fundraising was just beginning. It was still in an elementary stage and badly needed an injection of know how and professionalism. There was no existing organisation with the knowledge and experience to take an initiative. It was left, perhaps fortunately, for individuals at the grass roots to find a way forward by examining in more detail than the CUA authors had been able to do, the acknowledged source of best practice – the higher education sector in the United States.

It was to take another three years before an organised effort was made to bring North American expertise to bear on the nascent fundraising activities of British universities.

---

[17]   CUA Report, op. cit., pp. 70-71.

4

The growth of a UK/US partnership

US/UK links

The growing UK interest in US practice was paralleled by a similar interest from the US side in promoting fundraising in support of British higher education. Again individual initiatives made a difference. Gerald Burke, who was active in the Conference of University Administrators while serving in the Registrary's Office at the University of Cambridge, was a prime mover within the CUA and CASE to urge that US/UK scholarship exchange schemes should include administrators as well as academics in their programmes.

As a result, in 1982 CASE took part for the first time in the resulting Fulbright US/UK Administrative Exchange Program and a number of senior development directors from US universities who were CASE members subsequently spent a year in a UK university. Among the hosts were Leeds University 1983-84, Warwick 1984-85, Imperial College London 1986-87, The Open University 1987-88, and the University of Edinburgh 1987-88[1]. These exchanges provided opportunities for professional development both for the visitor and for staff in the UK university visited, for whom it was invariably the first opportunity they had had of meeting an experienced professional working in a field which was only slowly being recognised as a legitimate area of activity by university authorities in the UK. These personal links gave the UK hosts an idea of what was possible in the US, and provoked discussion on whether, and if so how, this experience might be adapted to suit UK conditions.

---

[1] Memo to Ad Hoc International Committee by Warren Heeman, 27 January 1989, 'Brief synopsis of CASE international activities'. CASE archives, Washington DC.

Similarly, a few individuals from UK universities had visited the US during the later 1980s to see how fundraising in universities was carried out. In 1989, in response to a growing interest on the part of CASE in extending its work internationally, a small group of UK professionals was invited to attend some CASE training events. They were Jo James (Lancaster), Keith Copland (Leeds), Ray Footman (Edinburgh) and Colin Boswell (Kent). These and a few others spread the word at grass roots in the UK about what US experience could do to help the struggling professionals emerging in university fundraising. Individual contacts like this began the process of 'technology transfer' whereby successful techniques for fundraising in US higher education were adapted and applied to UK conditions. This was possible because a growing and recognised need in UK universities for professional skills in this field coincided with a growing interest on the American side in exploring the possibilities for an international role for CASE.

The US participants in these exchanges were struck by the opportunities and potential offered by the UK university scene. This realisation was coupled with the insight that there was a near total failure on the part of UK academic leaders or their supporting administrators to grasp what was needed for successful fundraising in the higher education context. Without a credible UK partner CASE would be hard put to engage constructively with UK institutions. An experienced and sympathetic US observer, Warren Heeman, whilst a Fulbright scholar at Imperial College London in 1987, commented on the UK fundraising scene as he saw it:

I met with persons from many and varied institutions, some small and some large, some prestigious and some not, some with good fundraising potential and some it seemed to me with nothing running in their favour. But all had in common a paucity of fundraising experience and a painful lack of success. Several were beginning to feel something approaching panic, having been given an entirely arbitrary and unreasonable goal for the year [...] Several were told that they had to raise [funds for] their salary before anything else or their position would be discontinued [...] The closest any had to an alumni organisation were 'Old Student' societies, comprised in the main by those who had graduated thirty or more years ago and run entirely by the old students themselves. Their activity was limited to meeting for drinks and dinner once every year or so. Most colleges and universities had not communicated in any way with their former students, and, as a result, the institution had no record of where they were living – if, indeed, they were living. It was really tough in those days for those assigned the responsibility of raising money. What they needed – without reservation, without hesitation – was CASE.[2]

A UK partner for CASE

In September 1989 the Conference of University Administrators (CUA) followed up their 1984 booklet, 'Boosting University Income', by sponsoring a conference on fundraising and alumni relations at the University of Nottingham. Nottingham was a good choice since the new Vice-Chancellor, Sir Colin Campbell, was interested in development work (and was later to invest significantly in a fundraising programme). The conference was organised by Moyra Sutcliffe, the graduate liaison officer there. In her previous job as an alumni officer at the University of Sheffield, she had on her own initiative visited the University of Michigan at Ann Arbour and had been impressed by the positive way the Americans tackled alumni and fundraising work. She came back enthusiastic but conscious of the need to adapt what she had seen to the situation in the UK where the culture and scale of the work was very different. She welcomed the CUA approach to organise a programme.[3] Some thirty people came who were working in various capacities in the external relations field, including Warren Heeman, who was on a visit to the UK whilst serving as chair of the CASE board.

At the end of the conference an informal meeting was held to discuss how to follow up this initial gathering, resulting in the formation of an ad hoc committee. This was a self-selected group but broadly representative of higher education nationally including, as it did, universities and polytechnics (see Appendix A). It was clear to them that there was a national need to improve alumni and fundraising programmes and to raise the professional standard of those responsible. The quickest and most effective way to do this was to draw on US experience adapted as necessary to UK circumstances.

---

[2]   Extract from 'Statement on the Establishment of CASE UK' by Warren Heeman enclosed with letter dated 23 January 2009 from E.H. Byrd to J. Catlett, Director CASE Distinguished Service Awards. CASE archives, Washington DC.

[3]   Moyra Sutcliffe conversation with the author, 19 September 2012.

All those present were engaged in building up one or other of the components of a fundraising operation. Well aware of the shortage of experienced staff, they were focused on the need to train a team using the talented but inexperienced people available. Some at the Nottingham meeting had first hand experience of CASE; others were struck by the discovery of an organisation built on voluntary mutual self help, by people who were carrying the responsibility in their own universities for the activities they were talking about, and who had the experience and status to help others. As one participant at this original meeting said later: 'Anyone involved in alumni relations or fundraising knew that the real source of expertise lay in the United States and Canada.'[4]

Colin Boswell, then the development director at the University of Kent (and later the first executive director of CASE Europe), was one of the few that summer to attend a CASE event in the US. He circulated a paper, based on his experience at the fundraising course at Dartmouth NH, which recommended that the major role for CASE in the UK should be training. This was overwhelmingly the view of all present who, with only a few exceptions, had little or no experience of organising sustained fundraising operations. All recognised the urgent need to get up to speed themselves and to help other inexperienced staff to learn their own job by being exposed to the best practice proven elsewhere. It was unanimously decided to hold a training session – in CASE parlance an 'Institute' – in September of the following year, 1990. Ray Footman volunteered the University of Edinburgh as host; and he, Colin Boswell and Moyra Sutcliffe were asked to organise the programme. Warren Heeman undertook to secure the participation of some half a dozen experienced North Americans.

Several of those present were active in existing university professional organisations with broader aims. Neither they nor the rest of the ad hoc committee wanted to get into demarcation disputes with the Standing Conference of University Information Offices (SCUIO) or similar bodies. So it was decided that the programme would not include the usual PR track but concentrate on fundraising and alumni relations.

---

[4]   Ray Footman conversation with the author, 22 November 2011.

The Edinburgh Conference

The programme (see Appendix B), simple as it was, reflected exactly the preoccupations of the ad hoc committee. Despite their generally lowly status within their respective institutions, those involved needed to gain credibility with the university authorities by organising an intensive training programme which clearly showed that the new training venture was a positive contribution to raising standards and promoting efficiency. Thus the programme tackled the basic issues – Can North American experience be adapted and successfully transferred to a European context? What should the aims and objectives of an alumni relations programme be? What are the elements of a fundraising programme in a university? How do you start up an alumni relations or a fundraising programme on a small budget? The programme also included space and time for a Trade Exhibition at which for-profit firms relevant to the higher education market – software programs for databases, alumni merchandise, alumni publications and directories and consultants of all kinds – could show off their wares. This was another innovation in an academic world where words like 'marketing' and 'profit' still had the power to shock.

The Edinburgh Conference attracted over a hundred participants from all over the UK together with a handful from other European countries and a few from further afield, including two from Hong Kong. The relative inexperience and eagerness to learn was apparent from the opening session. At the first plenary session participants were asked how many had been working in the field for over five years? A few raised their hands. Over two years? A few more. Less than two years? Virtually the whole audience put their hands up.

The organisers were well aware of national sensitivities and that some university officials were cool towards the idea of 'the Yanks coming over and telling us how to do things'. More positively it was self evident that North American practice could not be simply transferred, given the differences in scale and in attitudes to fundraising within UK universities and their alumni constituencies. The programme was therefore structured so that an American and a UK professional were paired for each presentation.

It has to be said that what galvanised the participants was the style and attitude of the North American presenters. They were cheerful, positive, optimistic, professional and practical. Well aware of the differences of scale between development offices in the US and UK, they carried conviction because they were not preaching from the sidelines but talking as practitioners carrying the day to day responsibility. Their discussion of problems to be faced and how to overcome them was a revelation to many in the audience who had struggled in isolation with similar difficulties. For the first time many discovered that problems in their own institution were common problems, not the result of personal inadequacies; and that there were recognised ways of tackling them. Against the general air of scepticism in their home institutions, 'we began to realise', as one participant put it, 'that, yes, it could be done!'. And this explains the wave of enthusiasm the conference generated.

The other great advantage of the conference for many was the opportunity it offered to meet and learn, not only from the speakers, but from the other participants as well. Networking, though widely practised, was then a barely recognised phenomenon and the whole conference generated an atmosphere where the CASE ethos of volunteerism and mutual self help was dominant.

Another new dimension was the role of the private sector. For many of the university attendees this was the first time they had been able to see and compare the range of expertise the private sector had to offer in terms of specialised services and professional advice available to support their work. One such private sector participant, who attended the Edinburgh and many later CASE Europe conferences commented, 'The great potential for fundraising by UK universities was evident to me at Edinburgh in 1990. But it needed a whole new level of understanding within the sector, and time to build relationships with the leadership, before strategic consultants could be useful. This was to take another five years.'[5]

The CASE practice of having each session and each presenter evaluated by those present was important in maintaining standards and in ensuring the organisers were responsive to the needs of participants. The ad hoc committee, from the evaluation forms on the various presentations and their own observations, was

---

[5]   John G Glier, Chairman of Grenzebach Glier & Associates, a Chicago-based management consultancy in fundraising in the higher education, health and arts sectors. Conversation with author, 21 May 2013.

in no doubt that the conference had been a success and met a real need. This experience confirmed the committee's view that the best way to improve standards was to maintain and develop a close relationship with CASE in the US.

Given that Edinburgh showed such a conference was financially viable (it made a small surplus), the ad hoc committee decided to plan for a second conference in September 1991. Warren Heeman confirmed that CASE was willing again to participate. The University of Kent at Canterbury was available, so the date and venue for the following year were announced before the participants left Edinburgh.

Thus began an annual series of conferences which have continued to the present time. The expansion in the number of participants and the continued steady support from across the UK higher education sector and overseas showed that CASE Europe conferences met a real need in terms of university fundraising (see Appendix C).

Domestic institutional politics

Whilst the CASE board in Washington DC were working out the elements of an international policy, there were organisational changes in the UK bodies concerned.

The success of the initial conferences in Edinburgh and Kent had repercussions on the existing professional organisation of university information officers. During the first half of 1991 members of the Standing Conference of University Information Officers (SCUIO) let it be known that, as a result of the government's intention to merge universities and polytechnics,[6] SCUIO was planning its own merger with the Polytechnic Public Relations Information Services Conference (PPRISC) and would be extending membership to alumni relations and fundraising officers. The new organisation would be called the Higher Education External Relations Association (HEERA). At a joint meeting

---

[6]   By the Further and Higher Education Act 1992, polytechnics were freed from Local Authority control and made fully fledged universities with the power to award their own degrees.

of SCUIO and PPRISC in Oxford in September 1991 the merger was agreed and the first meeting of HEERA was held in October 1991 to approve a constitution. As a result of these developments, CASE HQ was asked not to pursue for the time being the question of a CASE office in London in case this prejudiced merger discussions with HEERA.[7]

The ad hoc committee had always been in favour of a single UK organisation. In this, the committee was mindful of the example of CASE in the US and its merger of related organisations in 1974, and of the experience of Canada which had recently formed the Canadian Council for Advancement of Education (CCAE) which represented those in alumni relations, fundraising and public relations in educational institutions in Canada. With this aim of institutional unity in mind, representatives of SCUIO had been invited to the Edinburgh Conference, and the ad hoc committee continued to explore the possibility of forming a single professional organisation covering the three areas of PR, alumni relations and fundraising.

The committee's discussion at Canterbury had the advantage of the presence of Marnie Spears, the Canadian president of CCAE.[8] Marnie was one of the North American presenters at the Kent Conference, and joined in the ad hoc committee's discussions about a possible merger of all related UK organisations. The discussion also benefited from reports from two members of the ad hoc committee who had attended the joint meeting of SCUIO and PPRISC.[9] As only a quarter of the participants at the joint SCUIO/PPRISC meeting (19 out of 72) had been from alumni relations or fundraising, it was felt that the representation of these two activities in the leadership of any new body should be strengthened. Not interested in trying to pursue a takeover of HEERA, the ad hoc committee was equally determined not to be taken over by an established group – many of whom had no interest in the new 'development' professionals

---

[7] Conclusion of CASE UK Ad Hoc Committee meeting at Nottingham on 24 May 1991 recorded in letter dated 28 May from C.W. Squire to Jeff Burnett at CASE HQ.CASE archives, Washington DC.

[8] Marnie Spears, Executive Director, Development and Public Relations at McMaster University, Ontario.

[9] Ray Footman, University of Edinburgh and Keith Copland, Development Director, University of Leeds; minutes of an informal meeting of the Ad Hoc Committee at the University of Kent, 17 September 1991.

– who had no expertise in the professional areas in which the UK group was most interested: alumni relations and fundraising.

The point was made that the Committee of Vice-Chancellors and Principals (CVCP) was highly supportive of HEERA, was concerned at the proliferation of professional training bodies, and would endorse HEERA over a CASE/UK or any other similar body. Despite these reservations, it was the unanimous view of the CASE/UK ad hoc committee that it should work for a single national organisation, provided this was not done at the expense of a close working relationship with CASE in the United States. The committee believed this to make sense in terms of efficiency and to be borne out by the separate experiences of colleagues in the US and in Canada where mergers had only come about after a good deal of inter-professional quarrelling. As a result the chair of the ad hoc committee wrote to the chair of HEERA proposing discussions between the two groups with a view to forming a single umbrella organisation. [10]

Over the next two years there were several meetings between representatives of the ad hoc committee and HEERA. A joint CASE UK/HEERA working party was set up and discussed details of the possible relationship between a national UK organisation and CASE in terms of affiliation fees, the provision of services on a cost basis and the administrative support of a London based CASE Europe office. At first these went well, with agreement in principle to draft a constitution to be put to their respective members for agreement by the autumn of 1992.[11] However, it soon became apparent there was a different perception of organisation goals: HEERA representatives saw their role as dealing with policy aspects of higher education and to educate the membership in the wider public affairs context. This was a somewhat more elevated role than the mundane concern of the CASE UK group, which was to concentrate on training to improve performance.

---

[10]   Letter dated 20 September 1991 from C.W. Squire, co-chair CASE UK ad hoc committee to Peter Reader, Chair of HEERA.CASE archives, Washington DC.

[11]   Report of second meeting of the joint working party CASE UK/HEERA on 18 February 1992 in letter dated 24 February 1992 from C.W. Squire to Jeff Burnett, CASE HQ.CASE archives, Washington DC.

By the time of the third conference at Lancaster in September 1992, it was clear that HEERA were no longer interested in a merger and intended to go it alone. This intention was never formally conveyed to the ad hoc committee and, after a period of nominal cooperation, the two organisations went their separate ways. Thus in the course of 1993 active negotiations with HEERA lapsed.

Yet the steady growth in demand for places at the annual training conferences reinforced the ad hoc committee's view that it was pursuing the right policy in securing a 'technology transfer' of best practice from North America, adapted by UK professionals to the UK context. Participants in the annual CASE/UK conferences had almost doubled from 127 at the first conference in Edinburgh to 248 in Cambridge three years later. It is currently running at over 600 participants each year (see Appendix C).

The ad hoc committee continued its discussions with CASE, the one organisation in a position to help the growing profession of alumni relations and university fundraising, over the provision of expertise in training, in particular for the annual conference. At the same time the group pursued a pragmatic policy of keeping a relationship with HEERA; CASE members were free to join HEERA and vice versa (a number of institutions and individuals had membership of both). The CASE/UK ad hoc committee had proposed to HEERA that a joint conference be organised in 1993 with HEERA responsible for the public information track. This proposal was agreed and from 1993 to 2002 the annual conference was badged as a HEERA/CASE conference, a collaboration which enabled the lapse of negotiations for a single organisation to close on a positive note. Thus although the objective of a single national organisation was not attained, a satisfactory modus vivendi was secured without ill will.

With the project of a single national organisation at an end, the ad hoc committee resumed discussions with CASE on the opening of an office in London to serve the UK and rest of Europe, which the committee was sure would improve the services CASE could provide, and ease the administrative burden on those universities which were hosting the annual CASE conference.

5
CASE and its international relationships

Planning an international policy

Despite the success of the 1990 Edinburgh Conference, it took three more years before the UK side was ready to enter a formal relationship with CASE and before the US side had worked out a formal international policy.

CASE's contacts with non-US educational institutions were of long standing, but on an ad hoc basis, rather than as a result of conscious policy. There had always been a strong Canadian membership of CASE, and Canadians were prominent amongst its elected volunteer leadership. International activities in the wider sense, however, had started only in the 1980s. Past presidents and chairs of the CASE board of trustees began to visit countries in Latin America, Europe and Asia to meet representative gatherings of higher education administrators, and college and university rectors, to speak about philanthropy, alumni administration and communications and educational fundraising. As early as September 1981 a senior CASE representative visited the UK and addressed the Conference of University Administrators. As has been seen above, CASE participation in the Fulbright exchange programme in the 1980s meant that a number of senior professionals were becoming familiar with UK conditions and opportunities.

Whilst still in the UK on his Fulbright year (1987), Warren Heeman began urging CASE to consider ways of helping professional colleagues in the UK who were struggling to get established. Heeman was at the time vice-president for PR and Development at the Georgia Institute of Technology, having served in a similar capacity at William and Mary College, Virginia. He was then a senior and experienced professional in his field. He was a quiet spoken individual, whose professional experience and a year's attendance at a UK higher educational establishment (Imperial College London ,1986-7) equipped him to adapt US practice to the UK academic environment. As a former trustee of CASE, he was also well placed to argue for a more active CASE policy in the international field. His influence as a former trustee was limited but, to his surprise, he was elected a second time to the CASE board, this time as Chair Elect designate for 1987-88, with the expectation (duly fulfilled) that he would be elected Chair for 1988-89. This put him in a strong position to lobby within CASE for the opening of a CASE office in the UK, despite strong reservations among some of his colleagues about an initiative of this kind.

In November 1988 the CASE board appointed a committee 'to review the questions and issues related to the concept of CASE/Europe'[1] with Warren Heeman as its chair. In April 1989 the committee produced a policy paper which reviewed the pros and cons of expanding CASE's international role and discussed the idea of opening a CASE office in London. The paper considered the idea of a London office premature, criticised the piecemeal approach to international activities which had characterised the CASE approach hitherto, and argued in favour of developing a clear policy and plan of action for CASE's international role. The choice was to leave well alone and to continue to service international members from the US through existing CASE activities in North America; or to prepare a long term plan for expanding CASE's outreach by establishing CASE offices in foreign countries. [2]

The arguments for the status quo were essentially practical: CASE had only just emerged from a period of major organisational expansion. Current and planned programmes were extensive. CASE needed to consolidate around these priorities before embarking on an international initiative which could overstretch the staff, and with financial implications which were far from clear. North American members might feel CASE was not well focused on the needs of its prime membership. Some might object to CASE resources derived from the domestic membership being used to support, in part, services to international members.

---

[1]   Memo to Ad Hoc International Committee, Warren Heeman, 27 January 1989. *Brief synopsis of CASE international activities* .CASE archives, Washington DC.

[2]   Paper by the Ad Hoc International Committee, 18 April 1989. *CASE's International Role and Responsibilities*. CASE archives, Washington DC.

The arguments for an expansion of CASE's international role were a mixture of idealistic and practical, but the driving motivation was to live up to CASE's role of 'helping educational institutions throughout the world [...] for the benefit of society'.[3] CASE had a global mission to support educational institutions worldwide by helping them to secure fiscal diversity and a measure of academic autonomy. In part it was a response to a competitive environment; non-profit groups similar to CASE, embryonic groups in other countries, as well as for-profit fund raising firms and consultants, were becoming active internationally. If CASE wanted to maintain its reputation and pre-eminent position in its chosen field it had to expand beyond its current borders, or lose ground to others. There were the further practical considerations that international linkages could provide advantages – professional experiences for CASE volunteers; and ultimately, perhaps, a source of revenue for CASE itself.

The committee recommended a study of the feasibility of a CASE Europe operation which could be a model for other areas of the world. Later the same year (1989) a working paper was produced summarising the phasing of the feasibility study with costings.[4] It envisaged two years for the study and related activities, followed by a three year start-up period for a CASE Europe office (CASE were already thinking in terms of a Europe-wide role for the new office). Total costs were estimated at US$1,228,125 of which roughly 75 per cent was to be raised from corporations and foundations, and the balance to be provided by CASE. It was evident that the idea of going international with the founding of a CASE Europe office meant a significant commitment of resources, and would require a serious UK interlocutor to be successful.

From the UK point of view a condition of financial dependence on the US organisation was not an advantageous situation. It was recognised that it would be highly desirable to achieve financial autonomy if the relationship in the longer term were to remain healthy. This was indeed to prove a source of friction over the years. Financial autonomy was eventually achieved though it took some ten years to get there.

---

3   *CASE's International Role and Responsibilities* op cit.
4   Working Paper (10 October 1989) *CASE in Europe: an overview for a feasibility study.* CASE archives, Washington DC.

Establishment of a CASE Europe office

The hiatus while the UK group sought to establish the practicality of a single UK-wide organisation in the external relations field risked, as Warren Heeman warned at the time, a loss of momentum at the US end.[5] Nevertheless, CASE continued to weigh the feasibility of establishing a local office to serve the needs of educational institutions throughout Europe on the basis of the 1989 feasibility study. The objective was to provide European institutions with the tools and skills 'to grow their own advancement programs and professional staff'. The original plan envisaged an initial phased two year programme (1989-91) in which a mixed US/UK task force evaluated the training needs of European education leaders and their institutions; and an evaluation of the legal and logistical basis for a small CASE office in London UK. This was to be followed by a fundraising phase, and then a three year start-up period (1991-94) for the CASE Europe office to become operational and self sustaining. This was not a decision to be taken lightly, for the feasibility study had estimated planning and three year start-up costs at US$1.25 million

Following the 1992 Lancaster Conference and the lapse of negotiations with HEERA, the UK group saw no further 'political' objection to pursuing the idea of a CASE Europe office in London. However, by this time the timetable for the establishment of an office had slipped. At the same time the value of the connection with CASE was reflected in the growth in the number of UK institutional members and in the size of the annual CASE conferences.

Institutional Membership of CASE for selected years (worldwide)[6]

	Membership worldwide	Of which UK Higher Education
1974	1835	Nil
1989	3204	5
1995	n/a	42
2000	n/a	74
2004 – 5	3082	119
2010 – 11	3418	145

---

[5]   Minutes of a meeting of the Canadian and International Services Task Force on 15 July 1991 at Montreal Quebec. CASE archives, Washington DC.

[6]   CASE Annual Reports.

The growth in the numbers (**Appendix C**) of those attending the annual conference was becoming a real burden on the development office of each host UK university. This lent more urgency from the UK end, since it was hoped that the establishment of a CASE office would assist in meeting this administrative need. The steady growth in attendance at the annual CASE UK conference reassured CASE HQ in Washington DC that an investment in their first overseas office would be a viable proposition.

By the time of the 1993 Cambridge Conference, attended by Peter Buchanan (the president of CASE) and Warren Heeman (former Chair of CASE board of trustees) as well as members of the CASE UK group (the old 'ad hoc committee' from 1989), there was general agreement that the time was ripe for CASE to make a formal move into the UK and the wider European scene. Peter Buchanan had secured the approval of the CASE trustees to underwrite the costs of the UK office. During the Cambridge Conference he approached Colin Boswell, then development director at the University of Kent, to become the first executive head of the proposed CASE Europe office in London. Colin Boswell had been one of the original four UK visitors to CASE in the US in 1989 and an original member of the CASE/UK ad hoc committee. He took up this new appointment in early 1994.

By the mid 1990s the grass roots movement for professional self improvement by development staff had consolidated into an organisation such that CASE HQ in Washington DC judged it worthwhile to invest in a European office with its own board of trustees, incorporated under English law as a charitable organisation. Just as those pioneers scattered nationally across the UK higher education scene were committed to spreading 'best practice' through training sessions at the annual conferences and through personal contact, so the purpose of the new charitable trust was 'to advance the education of fundraisers and administrators in the theory and practice of effective and efficient fundraising administration and alumni relations for the benefit of charitable educational institutions in the UK (later amended to Europe)'[7]. This exactly reflected the preoccupation of grass roots staff keen to develop a professional future, and of development directors charged with the responsibility of organising and

---

[7]   Deed of Declaration of Charitable Trust.6 October 1994.CASE archives, Washington DC.

managing a growing non-academic sector of higher education. It also exactly reflected the analysis of Warren Heeman seven years earlier after his Fulbright year at Imperial College London.

The work of CASE Europe

Inevitably the decision in principle to expand overseas and open a CASE Europe office in London necessitated a period of organisational build-up. The first director, Colin Boswell, took up his appointment in January 1994 and was initially preoccupied with legal issues and, less urgently, logistical matters of accommodation and staffing.

The legal structure for CASE (Europe) had to be settled so that it could operate as a charity under English law. A deed of trust was ultimately drawn up and came into effect in 1994 with initially three trustees, two from the UK and one from the US. CASE, as the 'founder', retained the power to remove trustees and thus to exercise ultimate control. Given the precarious dependence upon funds transferred from CASE, the new organisation grew slowly. The director initially worked from home and premises were first secured in 1995. Because of the growing attendance at the annual conference discussed above, CASE Europe took on a second member of staff in 1996 to relieve the administrative burden on the volunteer teams dealing with the substance of the conference programme.

In this early period (1994-2000) a number of one day events were organised, usually in London, on a variety of topics from the three major advancement areas: alumni relations, communications and PR, and educational fundraising. These used home grown talent but were sometimes built around an experienced North American practitioner who happened to be visiting. There were also budget priced events for support staff (administrative assistants, prospect researchers etc.) to give them an overview of what was meant by institutional advancement in terms of the breadth of work of a university development office, and how their job fitted in. Although CASE Europe focused mainly on higher education, its terms of reference covered schools too. Annual conferences covering both independent and maintained schools were initiated, and three were held in the period to 2000.

In addition, a number of events were organised in continental Europe (in Belgium, France, Germany and the Netherlands). The board of CASE Europe was also expanded to include representatives from continental European universities. This laid the basis for an expansion of CASE Europe's work in other European countries outside the UK, and was reflected in the growth in institutional membership in Europe.

European Institutional membership of CASE (higher education only)

Year	UK	Other Europe
1987	1	n/a
1988	3	n/a
1989	5	n/a
1990	24	n/a
1991	25	6
1995	42	10
2000	74	37
2005	119	69
2010	136	78
2011	145	80

Note: Figures for 1987-91 are taken from a working paper in CASE Archives, Washington DC, entitled 'CASE Canadian and International Services: History and Proposed Services', 15 April 1991

If the movement of ideas from the US to the UK required a culture shift in UK universities, a similar cultural shift was needed in the transfer of ideas to countries in continental Europe. The continental European universities at this time, both at staff and leadership level, were in most cases where UK universities had been ten years earlier. There were, in addition, linguistic barriers and policy differences from the situation in the UK e.g. over financing of higher education, student fees, the role of the state. This meant that CASE Europe needed to develop approaches that took account of these differences, and of the readiness or otherwise of the leadership of continental universities to contemplate new ideas of relationship building, alumni activities and fundraising. Broadly speaking, countries in Northern Europe (Scandinavia, The Netherlands, Belgium) were readier than others to consider these new areas of work. A number of universities from the continent attended CASE Europe conferences and became members of CASE. But this remains very much work in progress and an area of promise for the future.

These programmes filled a real need, but they still left CASE Europe short of revenue to be self-financing. Yet without more staff it was difficult to organise or market more events to generate more revenue. The steady growth in the participation in the annual CASE Europe conference (see Appendix C) and in institutional membership nevertheless showed that the demand was there and that CASE Europe was on the right track.

In the year 2000 Joanna Motion, formerly development director at the University of Kent, was appointed to succeed Colin Boswell. It was clear that the time frame envisaged by CASE HQ in Washington DC for CASE Europe to become self-financing was over-optimistic, and more time was needed than the three year start-up period initially envisaged. In March 2001 the main CASE board, under Scott Nichols, Dean of Development at Harvard Law School, was invited to meet the board of CASE Europe in Edinburgh. It became evident that the main board was determined that unless CASE Europe could break even, the policy of financial support from Washington DC would be reviewed. There was therefore an urgent need to supplement revenue-generating activities. The new director of CASE Europe decided to explore more actively the possibility of support from charitable organisations interested in CASE's work in improving the fundraising capacity of UK universities.

Shortly after her appointment, Joanna was introduced to Michael Gwinnell, a representative of Atlantic Philanthropies, a charitable foundation funded by Chuck Sweeney, a publicity-shy Irish American philanthropist, who had supported the higher education and other social and human rights programmes in Ireland, north and south, from the 1980s onwards. Higher education in the island of Ireland benefited by some 750 million euro from Sweeney's philanthropy, which leveraged many millions more from government and other sources.[8]

---

[8]   Cullen, P. (2012) 'Atlantic Philanthropies. Third-level sector biggest beneficiary of Atlantic's funds'. *Irish Times*. 10 July 2012.

It had long been recognised by universities wanting to start a fundraising operation that there was (and still is) a serious shortage of able and experienced home-grown talent for senior posts in university development offices. The foundation had already supported some individual educational institutions in their efforts to start fundraising. So CASE Europe developed a proposal for an intensive training programme over a one to two week period for young professionals with some experience, designed to equip them for posts of greater responsibility. Atlantic Philanthropies saw in the proposal an opportunity to leverage its support to higher education, since by funding a training programme attended by a number of universities it could achieve a multiplier effect through the improvement in understanding and efficiency of participants when they returned to their own institutions or moved on to posts of greater responsibility elsewhere.

Atlantic Philanthropies therefore made a substantial grant for the start-up and related costs of running what became an annual event. The first session was held in 2002 and has continued annually ever since. These training sessions, based originally in the University of Durham and now at Loughborough, were limited in the number of participants to ensure a good staff/student ratio. They were quickly recognised as highly successful in preparing younger professionals for posts of greater responsibility. Once established, the course became a significant source of revenue for CASE.

In parallel, participation at annual CASE conferences continued to grow and, with HEERA and CASE Europe going their separate ways after 2002, the organisation, revenue and costs of the annual conference became the sole responsibility of CASE Europe. By 2004 the finances of CASE Europe were on an even keel with the organisation at last breaking even, ten years after its establishment. By achieving financial autonomy CASE Europe was relieved of a good deal of pressure from CASE HQ and had vindicated the faith of those who had seen how the ideals and practice of CASE could be adapted successfully in a non-American environment.

By this time CASE Europe and its role in training and spreading the best practice had become well known in university circles. Vice-Chancellors were becoming more engaged in external relations, and more familiar with their own role in fundraising. As a result the board of CASE Europe was strengthened by the appointment of some vice-chancellors as trustees, notably Professor Sir David Williams (ex-Cambridge) 2002-05, Professor Sir Duncan Rice (Aberdeen) 2005-10, Professor Eric Thomas (Bristol) 2007 to date, and Professor Shirley Pearce (Loughborough) 2009 to date. This showed the progress made in the professionalisation of fundraising and its integration at policy level within universities. The involvement of vice-chancellors was to prove critical in the subsequent evolution of government policy.

6
The involvement of vice-chancellors

Background

> 'Philanthropic support for higher education in the United Kingdom is
> not new, nor even recent. Almost every UK degree-awarding institution
> whose lineage is older than the middle of the twentieth century was
> founded and grew on the shoulders of philanthropic support.'[1]

The post-war history of university fundraising shows that every successful
operation has involved the active participation of the vice-chancellor and other
leading academics. Yet, with few exceptions, vice-chancellors took little interest
in the subject from the end of World War II to the end of the twentieth century.
It is at first surprising that British academics, many of whom were familiar with
the US scene, and aware of the role philanthropy had played in many US
universities, should have ignored such a valuable source of funds. Universities
UK (the professional organisation of vice-chancellors and principals of
universities and colleges) and its predecessor bodies up to the end of the
millennium never took an initiative on fundraising either to oppose or
encourage it.[2] The main explanation of this neglect, as has been shown earlier,
was simple: for much of the second half of the twentieth century there was no
need to. There was in British politics bipartisan agreement to fund a major
expansion of higher education by taxation. University administrators focused
on various governmental funding streams, first by ensuring they took their full
quota of students (student numbers were 'capped' to +/- 5% on the previous

---

[1] HEFCE *Review of Philanthropic Support for Higher Education (2011-12) Introduction to
the Consultation*. hefcereview@morepartnership.com.

[2] Conversation with Lady Diana Warwick (Chief Executive of UUK 1995-2009), 5
July 2012.

year, and some administrators deliberately aimed to go 5% over every year).
Then there were important capital grants available, but which had to be bid for.
Here the research assessment exercise (RAE) conducted by government at
regular intervals was important. The better a department's RAE assessment, the
better the chances of further funding. But the political commitment to fund
expansion in student numbers did not keep pace with the financial need.

Increasingly too vice-chancellors looked beyond government sources, notably
to entrepreneurial initiatives for company-sponsored research or special courses
designed for particular industries or sectors. Also notable was the way
universities expanded their recruitment of foreign students. These were not
part of the 'cap' (the government ceiling on the numbers of UK and later EU
students supported by public funds) since they were not funded by the
government, and universities were free to set fees according to the full costs of
the course.

These factors do not wholly explain the neglect of fundraising in the period
down to the mid-eighties. There were cultural and generational reasons too:
the academic leadership was by this time drawn from the post war generation
who had themselves benefited from a free university education. Although it
was in order to receive a benefaction, the British were inhibited about asking
for money, even for an institutional benefaction; it was felt to be *infra dig.* and
un-British at a personal level to cultivate an acquaintanceship with a view to
soliciting for funds.

There was also a natural reluctance at a time of pressure on resources to make
the financial investment needed to set up a fundraising arm, which would have
diverted funds from academic activities. Furthermore, some academics
questioned the need for such professional fundraising. Surely philanthropists
would find their own way, or be drawn in by star academics, without the need
for a fundraising bureaucracy? This sort of complacency was not justified by
the rate of inflow of philanthropic funds. Moreover, such an attitude
misunderstood the role of the fundraiser in the university context. This role
was to support academics by bringing the scholarly and scientific work of the
university to the attention of potential donors, to introduce the latter where
needed to the academics concerned and to do any administrative follow up.
Whilst high quality scholars and scientists attracted philanthropists, these

academics rarely had the time to devote to finding and cultivating potential donors; most welcomed the idea that this 'housekeeping' side of fundraising would be taken off their shoulders, and their time concentrated on the critical role of presenting and explaining their work to potential donors.

Academic culture is anyway anti-management. Managers are regarded as getting in the way; they restrict freedom of action by enforcing budgetary control and other non-academic requirements. In addition, management is perceived as a cost centre with a strong propensity to grow for no very good reason, diverting resources away from academic priorities. So, although fundraising was a revenue centre, not a cost centre, this could only be demonstrated when the initial investment had yielded a positive return. At the point of decision – whether to invest resources in a fundraising programme or not – internal academic opinion was invariably sceptical, if not hostile.

Furthermore, unlike some management areas such as health and safety, equal opportunities, and other personnel issues, there was no legislative backing to oblige universities to engage in fundraising. It would require leadership from the top of the university to earn the understanding and support for a new activity which, whatever its theoretical promise, meant initially a reduction in resources available for academic work.

There was the additional consideration that outside support for academic work, notably research sponsored by corporate donors, could give rise to conflicts of interest. It was left largely to the good sense of the individual department to negotiate satisfactory arrangements with outside donors within generally accepted guidelines. The terms of engagement were not only a matter of ethics over the source of funds but also involved questions of intellectual property, freedom to publish and wider issues of academic independence. So long as such cases were relatively few, university administrators dealt with them on an ad hoc basis. As and when universities began serious investment in fundraising such an ad hoc approach risked being sometimes proved inadequate (as will be seen later – see Chapter 8) and more formal arrangements were then needed.

By the 1990s many leaders in the higher education sector had long been grappling with the need to diversify and expand revenue sources other than from the government. A number of universities had begun to invest in the organised pursuit of private gifts by appointing development staff and initiating fundraising programmes. There had, however, been little collective discussion of the policy issues involved - the role of vice-chancellors and principals, the scale of resources required, or of the results obtained or to be expected. The national bodies representing vice-chancellors and principals were too big for the kind of informal discussion of the sensitive issues involved.

The need for vice-chancellors and principals to be engaged more deeply in the business of fundraising was evident. If the personal participation of the head of the institution was essential for successful fundraising, it was important that he or she should be well informed about what role to play, and when involvement at leadership level should take place. It was also needful for the morale, and hence the effectiveness, of the internal team; above all it was essential for engaging the interest of potential benefactors – if the leadership was not committed, why should outsiders take it seriously?

In addition, there were national issues where the weight of opinion of a group of vice-chancellors could be important, for instance in encouraging poorer institutions to commit resources to raising private gifts; or in influencing government policy on fresh incentives for the charity sector as a whole through the tax system. An active policy of self-help through policies of charitable fundraising was a better basis for a constructive dialogue with the government than unimaginative and repetitious demands for more funds from the public purse, demands which might ultimately damage vice-chancellors' relations with government ministers.

By the late 1990s there was a group of universities whose vice-chancellors had taken the risk of publicly committing scarce resources to starting up a fundraising operation. Most vice-chancellors had some experience of dealing with one or two major donors; few had experience of leading a major and sustained fundraising campaign. Nor had they experience of what scale of resources they should commit to fundraising or of the returns to be expected over what period. They were all vulnerable to criticism from within their universities if expenditure on fundraising and related activities turned out to be disproportionate to the funds raised. Unhappily there were no comparative data, since each university considered these figures too sensitive to be made public.

Two vice-chancellors with experience of US universities, and committed to an active fundraising policy in their own institutions, were Professor David VandeLinde, vice-chancellor of the University of Bath, and Professor Duncan Rice, principal and vice-chancellor of the University of Aberdeen. David VandeLinde was an American, and had served as dean of engineering at Johns Hopkins before coming to Bath as vice-chancellor (1992-2001) and subsequently Warwick (2001 – 2006). Duncan Rice was an Aberdonian and a graduate of Aberdeen, but had spent much of his academic career in the US, serving as vice-chancellor of New York University (1991-1996) before returning to Aberdeen as principal and vice-chancellor (1996-2010). He had startled his staff and the audience at his inaugural speech on taking up office by announcing his intention to run a fundraising campaign (ultimately successful) for £100 million, a target unprecedented in Scotland at the time. Both thought that a private and informal discussion of such issues in a peer group selected by them, but nationally representative, would be valuable[3]. The two vice-chancellors agreed to act as co-chairmen at an initial meeting sponsored by Grenzebach Glier Europe. John Glier, the CEO of the parent company and a well-known figure in the charitable fundraising world in the US, had established that Professor Frank Rhodes, president emeritus of Cornell University, was willing to attend the meeting and take part in the discussion. Professor Rhodes was born in England and was a graduate of the University of Birmingham, having held academic appointments in the University of Wales, Swansea, and then at the University of Michigan (1968 – 1977) before becoming president of Cornell (1977 – 2000). He was low key, quietly spoken with an impressive record as a fundraiser. The idea was that vice-chancellors would be more receptive to ideas coming from an equal than from professional staff or consultants. Moreover, this was an opportunity for them to discuss complex issues with colleagues in a private forum and to hear the views and experience of their peers in a new and expanding area of activity. All three men were familiar with the cultural differences between the US and the UK, and were well placed to judge how best to adapt US fundraising practice to the UK context.

The initial meeting of this ad hoc group of vice-chancellors in September 1999

---

[3]   The existence of this group of vice-chancellors is mentioned in DfES Task Force Report to Government (May 2004), *Increasing Voluntary Giving to Higher Education*. Chapter 2, p. 18. (The Thomas Report).

attracted ten heads of institutions and two deputies (see Appendix F). The presence of Professor Rhodes proved a catalyst and led to useful formal and informal discussions. The value of the meeting was evident from the fact that participants agreed to meet again. Eventually eleven meetings in all were held over a period of seven years, with an average attendance of nine to ten. Sometimes an outside visitor was invited to join the discussions, someone who could bring experience of a particular aspect of philanthropy and give a different perspective on fundraising.[4] The meetings were hosted by a member of the group, latterly Professor Malcolm Grant, provost of University College London, and staffed and supported by Grenzebach Glier Europe.

From the start, the group were action-orientated. No minutes were taken, but points for action were circulated after each meeting. At this first meeting, the group initiated action on two issues – the tax treatment of philanthropic gifts, and data collection - which required follow-up and had some important consequences in later years.

Charity taxation

Earlier in the year (1999), HM Treasury had circulated a consultation document[5] as part of a once in ten years review of charity taxation, inviting comments from interested parties. Cambridge and one or two other universities had done some work on this but had decided not to submit unilateral comments. Although the deadline for submission of comments had passed by the time of the vice-chancellors' meeting in September, the Treasury indicated that a late submission, if received by the end of October, would be considered.

The topic of the taxation of charitable gifts was on the group's agenda and Paul Judge, a trustee of the Cambridge Foundation and a major donor to Cambridge,

---

[4] In addition to Frank Rhodes, these included Paul Judge, a major donor to Cambridge, Will Wyatt, a director of BBC Television and later President of the Royal Television Society, and William Richardson, President and CEO of the WK Kellogg Foundation and a former president of Johns Hopkins University.

[5] HM Treasury (March 1999) *Review of Charity Taxation : A Consultation Document.* London: HMSO.

introduced the discussion with John Quelch, then dean of the London Business School. A draft was circulated within ten days of the meeting which drew on work already done by the Cambridge Foundation and by John Craven, chairman of the Deutsche Morgan Grenfell Group (and another Cambridge trustee). This draft was approved and signed by fourteen vice-chancellors or deputies and seven lay leaders from the higher education sector before the end of October and in time to affect the Treasury announcement on 9 November 1999 on 'Getting Britain Giving in the 21st Century'.[6]

Tax incentives for charitable giving cover a much wider field than higher education, and cannot be considered except in the general context of charitable giving nationally. Although individual vice-chancellors, the ad hoc group and, later on, the Thomas Report, continued to argue for the general improvement of incentives to charitable giving, this was not an area in which they could have a decisive impact, and it remains 'work in progress'. Nevertheless the group continued to keep up a correspondence with Treasury ministers, collected data on donors who had taken advantage of the improvements in the tax regime for charitable gifts set out in the Budget for 2000, and continued to argue in favour of extending tax relief to unquoted shares and securities. In 2002 the group also raised the possibility in the longer term of a tax regime for 'planned giving' on the US model where the donor retains a life interest in the asset irrevocably donated, a proposal again recommended in the Thomas Report of 2004 (see Chapter 7).

Successive governments have maintained a generally positive attitude to philanthropic giving to UK charities. The budget proposals of 2012, proposing a cap on tax relief for charitable donations, now fortunately withdrawn, aroused some disquiet at the time. Though tax relief is not generally regarded as a primary motive in charitable giving, any philanthropist will wish to choose a tax-efficient means. The economic austerity policies following the global financial crisis of 2008 were not propitious for new tax incentives, though discussion continues on possible changes in the tax regime to encourage voluntary giving throughout the charitable sector.

------

[6]   HM Treasury (1999) Getting Britain Giving in the 21st Century. Pre-Budget Report, 9 November 1999.

Gift revenue and fundraising costs

"Thou shalt not muzzle the ox when he treadeth out the corn"[7]

A more fruitful area of discussion and one in which the vice-chancellors' group was to have a direct impact, both on their own management of fundraising activities and on government policy, was the collection of data on fundraising costs and gift revenue. In particular there was a need to establish how much a given fundraising programme might be expected to cost, and what returns might be expected. This was discussed at the very first meeting in 1999 when it was noted that there were no comparative data available, and none were being collected. The group were unanimous that it would greatly help rational discussions about the level of resources needed for fundraising in UK circumstances if such data were available. This would also be helpful in evaluating the performance of fundraising programmes, as well as in dealing with internal critics.

There were complex questions of definitions to be settled, but the group were clear it was essential to begin the process of data collection, recognising the necessity to extend and improve it in due course. In September 1999 the vice-chancellors of Aberdeen and Bath, as co-chairmen, and the rector of the London Institute (now the University of the Arts) volunteered their development directors[8] to design a questionnaire for circulation. The trio were authorised to consult CASE Europe to see if they could supply some administrative support, and were given the (unrealistic) timeframe of agreeing and circulating a questionnaire by Christmas 1999, with the results to be collated by March 2000 at an overall cost of £5.6 million. In the event, whilst the original questionnaire was duly circulated, it was to take the respondent development directors some time to compile their replies. As a result the first ever report on gift data and fundraising costs covering ten UK universities[9] was presented to the vice-chancellors' group in June 2001. This showed that, for the ten universities

---

[7]   Deuteronomy 25:4.

[8]   These were Caroline Underwood, London Institute (now University of the Arts), Ben Morton Wright, University of Aberdeen and Robert Gordon, University of Bath.

[9]   The pioneer universities were Aberdeen, Bath, Durham, Edinburgh, London Institute, Nottingham, Oxford, UCL, Warwick and York.

reporting, a total of £40.8 million had been raised in 1999-2000. The amounts raised by each university varied from £186,600 to £16.9 million.

Vice-chancellors present recognised that this was a pilot survey and decided that it should be repeated in the following year, inviting additional universities to take part. This time seventeen universities took part, reporting for 2001-02 a total £105 million raised at an overall cost of £12.5 million.[10] To improve the quality of the data so that all respondents were working to the same definitions, it was decided to refine the guidelines for the questionnaire. This was not really a matter for vice-chancellors and the group referred this task to their development directors as being within their expertise. The decision to involve development directors in the work of the group, and the readiness to turn to CASE for back-up, were of significance for the future. These decisions helped to involve vice-chancellors more closely with their development directors and with CASE, to the benefit of successful fundraising nationally.

The vice-chancellors' group continued to meet and discuss such topics as the recruitment and retention of senior fundraising staff, training (including for vice-chancellors and senior lay volunteers), and to support specific initiatives by CASE (Europe) and others in these fields. But by 2007 the issues the group had originally been set up to discuss had become mainstream and were regularly discussed within Universities UK and with government departments. The purpose of the group had therefore been fulfilled and it dissolved itself after eight years of existence.

The Ross Group

In 2000, a little later than the first meeting of the vice-chancellors' group, an informal, self-selected group of development directors had begun meeting to discuss matters of common concern in what was initially called the development directors' forum. Membership was by invitation and deliberately limited to individuals (not institutions) recognised by their peers as 'responsible for significant development programmes'. The original members included

---

[10]   Thomas Report, op. cit. Chapter 2, para 13, and unpublished survey by vice-chancellors' ad hoc group, circulated at the 6th meeting on 29 October 2002. The survey's authors were four development directors: Mary Blair (LSE), Michelle Calvert (Aberdeen), Alistaire Lockhart (UCL) and Jon Walker (Loughborough).

Aberdeen, Birmingham, Bristol, Cambridge, Durham, Edinburgh, Glasgow, KCL, Kent, Loughborough, LSE, Manchester, Nottingham, Oxford, Queen's Belfast and UCL. This group was larger than and independent of the vice-chancellors' group but the two groups naturally complemented each other.

At the third formal meeting of the development directors' forum in March 2003 at Ross Priory on Loch Lomond, part of the University of Strathclyde, it was agreed that, for purposes of external representation and for the better conduct of business, the group should elect a chairman to serve for one year and to arrange and issue agendas for meetings. It was also decided to rename the forum the Ross Group and to meet twice a year, once at Ross Priory and once elsewhere in the UK. The executive director of CASE Europe (Joanna Motion) was invited to attend. Thus three active groups were working in parallel to promote better practice in fundraising throughout the higher education sector – the vice-chancellors' ad hoc group, the Ross Group and CASE Europe – and, although independent of each other, became functionally linked.

At its June 2001 meeting, the vice-chancellors' group had invited the development directors' forum to help refine the guidelines for the survey of gift revenue and fundraising costs. This was followed by the group's decision to invite all universities who had attended meetings of the ad hoc group or of the development directors' forum (thus showing a serious interest in fundraising) to participate in the 2002 survey. In this way the survey was extended from the original ten to some twenty-four universities. The director of CASE Europe was invited to take part in the exercise to relieve development directors of the administrative task of processing the replies.

Because of the evident value of the data collected, there then developed a regular pattern in which the co-chairmen of the vice-chancellors' group wrote an annual letter to their fellow vice-chancellors inviting them to take part in the survey. The approach at vice-chancellor level was decided on to emphasise the policy need for such data. The survey itself continued to be based on guidelines and questionnaires continually refined by the development directors who were members of the Ross Group. [11] As more and more universities joined in the

---

[11]　See Appendix H, Participation in annual survey of gift revenue costs (Ross/CASE Survey).

survey, so the burden of processing became heavier and was eventually outsourced. But it remained closely supervised by a working group of development directors which in 2002 consisted of Michelle Calvert (Aberdeen), Mary Blair (LSE), Jon Walker (Loughborough), Alisdaire Lockhart (UCL) and Joanna Motion (CASE Europe). The survey, now called the Ross Survey (after the development directors' group), has been repeated every year since. By 2004 some eighty universities were invited to participate and it later became a condition of government financial support for fundraising that any university seeking such support (e.g. through the matched funding scheme, see Chapter 7 below) should take part in the survey. It is now an irreplaceable source of national data in the HE sector.

Again it is worth noting the serendipity of two independent self selected groups in the university world, one at the policy level, one at the working level, coming together to support each other's work and compiling a product of value not just to themselves, but to the entire higher education sector and to central government. The data the survey produced helped show the effect of government incentives in increasing voluntary giving to higher education, hence in turn influenced government policy by showing that such incentives, if introduced more widely, had a good chance of being successful.

At the end of the twentieth century only about 20 per cent of higher education institutions had initiated fundraising programmes. It had taken over fifteen years since the CUA report on 'Boosting University Income' to secure this level of participation. Nevertheless the activities of the vice-chancellors' group at the policy level, the work of the Ross Group at the professional level and the work of CASE in training and raising awareness had prepared the way for a major expansion. So when the government took a practical initiative to encourage more fundraising, universities were in a position to respond.

7
Governmental initiatives

The missing link

By the turn of the millennium, more and more vice-chancellors were accepting their critical role in fundraising; development directors, with the help of CASE Europe, were training new staff and improving professional standards. Meanwhile, at national level, a political debate continued with growing heat over the best means of funding the expansion of higher education. This was a major issue for the Labour government of the day, which had made a commitment in its 2001 election manifesto not to allow universities to increase tuition fees. The then prime minister, Tony Blair, commenting on the New Labour domestic reforms, wrote that 'perhaps the most fiercely contested was the change to university funding'. [1]

The debate focused on whether to increase student fees or introduce a graduate tax. Charles Clarke, who became Secretary of State for Education and Skills in November 2002, delayed the planned White Paper on 'The Future of Higher Education' for two months whilst he undertook an urgent review of the options. Clarke argued that there were three beneficiaries of the higher education system: the state, the employer and the individual. It was common to all that central government would continue to maintain core funding. The question was how could the other two beneficiaries – the employer and the individual – make their contribution? Theoretically employers of graduates could pay an increased National Insurance contribution; and graduates could make their contribution through an addition to their income tax. As far as equity was concerned, the graduate tax placed the burden on those who benefited. But to increase a university's financial autonomy these contributions would have to be

---

[1] Blair, T (2010) *A Journey*. London: Hutchinson. P. 481.

hypothecated back to the individual's own university, otherwise they would be collected by central government and reallocated at the discretion of the centre. The Inland Revenue objected on practical grounds to the complications involved in hypothecation. According to Clarke[2], the Chancellor of the Exchequer said he favoured a graduate tax but did not want to introduce it in the current parliamentary session, where other major changes in taxation were planned.

The prime minister, Tony Blair, was convinced that the overall financial position of the university sector was unsustainable on the current model, and that there was an urgent need to get more funds into UK universities during the current parliament. However, he did not like the idea of a general tax on graduates dependent on their income, since 'it amounted not to a personal repayment of a personal debt, but a general graduate repayment of the collective student debt'.[3] He believed that the dominant position of US universities was due in part to their system of fees. Hence it was decided to increase tuition fees through a scheme whereby the government provided income to universities equal to the fee levels the universities set (from zero to £3,000 at the discretion of each individual university); government would recoup the cost over time through a student loans scheme, but only when a student was earning a minimum salary. This was coupled with special help for poorer students.

Against the background of this major debate, the encouragement of university fundraising was a relatively minor theme, given that it could make little immediate impact on the current financial situation of universities. But ministers recognised its long term potential, both in increasing the resources available to universities and in promoting their autonomy.

The 2003 White Paper broke new ground in specifically endorsing fundraising as a proper activity for universities: 'The government will continue to be the major funder of universities but they should also have greater freedom to access new funding streams on their own account.'[4] It repeated this message in the other sections: 'If we are to give (the universities) real freedom, we must look at ways of helping our universities change the culture of giving and lever in

[2]   Conversation with the author, 8 March 2012.
[3]   Blair, T. op. cit., p. 487.
[4]   DES. (2003) *The Future of Higher Education. Cmnd.* 5735, London: HMSO. p.8.

more funding of their own'.[5] And again: 'We need to ensure that we have a culture of giving in which donors and all our institutions (of higher education) including those with no history of incentivising donations, make the most of the potential of endowment. We want to build the culture of giving.'[6]

The White Paper committed the Department for Education and Skills for a limited period to find resources for 'matched endowment funding'.[7] Compared with the highly controversial decision to raise tuition fees, the references to encouraging 'a culture of giving' and 'endowment' – shorthand for fundraising – were almost throwaway lines. But they encapsulated a governmental decision for the first time ever to offer financial support to encourage universities to implement fundraising policies.

Although much university opinion remained open-minded in the face of these announcements, there were still academic critics who dismissed fundraising as no answer to the funding gap. Refering to the 2003 White Paper, one review commented: 'The emphasis on endowment funding is whistling in the dark. The DfES cannot simply wave a magic wand to transfer UK culture into US culture.'[8] It is fair comment that fundraising is not a complete solution to the financial needs of UK higher education but it is incontrovertible that it can make a significant contribution to an institution's finances. And subsequent developments were to prove this critic wrong in dismissing the ability of the sector to learn from US experience, and to build a growing revenue stream by a more professional approach to fundraising.

The timing of the White Paper's financial commitment, fortuitous perhaps, could not have been better. The pioneer work of a few individuals and universities in initiating fundraising on a more professional basis, the role of CASE Europe in training staff, the formation of the Ross Group of development directors, and the gradual process whereby a growing number of vice-chancellors became better informed and involved, meant that the human

---

5   Ibid., Section 1.36.
6   Ibid.,Section 7.17.
7   Ibid.,Section 7.18.
8   Centre for Philosophical and Religious Studies, Department of Theology and Religious Studies, University of Leeds.

understanding and (just) enough professional expertise were available to take advantage of the government scheme to spread fundraising capacity across the sector. By reducing the financial risk for universities, the government's scheme ultimately enabled almost the entire higher education sector to take the plunge and try their hand at fundraising. In 2003 some twenty-nine higher education institutions (HEIs) reported fundraising data for the Ross-CASE survey. By the end of the new government programmes considered below, the number of HEIs covered by 2010-11 survey had risen to over 160[9]. This impressive expansion of fundraising activity arose from a seminal report by a small group set up by the government under the chairmanship of a serving vice-chancellor.

The Thomas Report[10]

In July 2003, as foreshadowed in the White Paper, the Department of Education and Skills set up a task force to report on ways of increasing voluntary giving to higher education. In accordance with the government's policy of seeking to engage the university world directly, a serving vice-chancellor, Professor Eric Thomas, of the University of Bristol, was chosen as the chair of the task force.

Professor Thomas was appointed vice-chancellor in 2001 yet at his various interviews in the selection process he was asked no questions about fundraising. He later said this was perhaps fortunate since he had had 'nothing to do with fundraising till I went to Bristol'.[11] Bristol was one of the early universities to start a fundraising operation and in 1991 had set up a 'Campaign for Change' with a modest £10 million target over a ten year period. There was thus an environment of fundraising at Bristol, and the forthcoming centenary of the University's charter in 2009 was to be the occasion of a new campaign – hence his interest in fundraising which, up till then, had been 'quite passive', and his readiness to chair the government taskforce.

---

[9] National Centre for Social Research (2012) *Giving to Excellence : generating philanthropic support for UK Higher Education 2010-2011* (23 March 2012) [online] https://rosscasesurvey.org.uk/.

[10] "Increasing voluntary giving to higher education" Task Force report to government, May 2004 (The Thomas Report), Department for Education and Skills, reference TFVG2HE052004

[11] Conversation with the author, 1 March 2012.

The other members each brought different expertise and experience to the task. Sir Peter Lampl, who had been chairman of a private equity firm operating in the US and UK, was an active philanthropist through the Sutton Trust, an educational charity he established in 1997; he was familiar with US attitudes to fundraising, and had an interest in charitable tax reform. Tom Hughes-Hallett was at the time chief executive of Marie Curie Cancer Care, after a career in banking, and was experienced in the wider charity scene outside higher education. Dr Mary Blair was an American who had served in the development office of John Hopkins and its medical school and since 2000 had been the development director of the London School of Economics. She brought her 'hands-on' experience of managing a fundraising operation in a UK academic environment.

As part of the process of gathering data, some members of the taskforce went on a fact finding mission to the United States to visit a range of higher education institutions. The presence on the fact finding mission of three additional vice-chancellors from City, Lancaster and Teeside universities meant that the lessons of the US visit, ultimately embodied in the report itself, would be personally disseminated and gain added weight from the first-hand experience of a number of vice-chancellors. For the experience of the state/publicly funded universities in America gave the lie to a common argument amongst the 'do nothing' leaders in some UK institutions, that Oxford and Cambridge/the Russell Group[12] universities were in a different world whose experience in fundraising had no relevance for others. The taskforce, on the contrary, saw plenty of evidence that successful fundraising was not the preserve of the private Ivy League universities, but that state universities and other publicly funded institutions of higher education had also developed successful programmes: 'Many public universities (in the US) have succeeded over the last 20 years in significantly increasing the money that they raise from voluntary giving.'[13]

The task force had been asked to advise the government on how to promote giving to the higher education sector; how to sustain such giving through a change in culture within universities and the wider public; and potential

---

[12] The Russell Group comprises 24 leading research and teaching universities from all parts of the UK.

[13] The Thomas Report, op.cit, Chapter 3, para 18.

changes to the tax system to support increased giving. On the last point – tax treatment of charitable giving – the report made a series of suggestions[14] which, since they affected the whole charitable sector, have become part of an ongoing dialogue with the Treasury, and other departments directly concerned.

A central recommendation of the report was the need to create an 'asking' culture, on the premise that 'the most effective method of raising donations is to ask for them'.[15] From this simple premise flowed a series of corollaries which hitherto had been scarcely articulated, still less fully understood and acted upon. They included the fact that successful fundraising was not the sole province of the fundraisers but required the active involvement of the vice-chancellors, academics, lay governors, as well as the development staff, in creating relationships with potential benefactors; the recognition that a realistic timeframe for practical results was measured by years, not months; and by treating the embryo development office and its staffing not as a cost centre to be kept at a minimum, but as a revenue centre to be strengthened .

Other suggestions for action by higher education institutions included the novel idea that the job description of a vice-chancellor and other institutional leaders should be amended to give greater prominence to development work. For governing bodies to accept that a vice-chancellor should devote x days a year to fundraising duties required a large advance in understanding. Many governing bodies to date had avoided the need to make any allowance for this additional activity, hoping that time for fundraising (often requiring foreign travel and high profile public events) could just be fitted in to a vice-chancellor's schedule. The failure to make specific provision for vice-chancellors to delegate more of their duties to make space for these extended requirements was a serious disincentive to busy vice-chancellors to make the time commitment required for successful fundraising.

The report also picked up the revolutionary suggestion in the 2003 White Paper that government was ready to move from exhortation to action, by recommending 'a matched funding scheme to support institutions' capacity building for effective fundraising [...] and to follow this with a matched funding scheme for donations'.[16]

---

[14]   The Thomas Report, op. cit., Chapter 5.
[15]   Thomas Report, op. cit, p. 27.
[16]   The Thomas Report, op. cit., Recommendation 11, p.10.

The economic climate for public expenditure in 2004 was favourable since the global economic crisis did not become apparent until 2008. So, if the will was there, it was relatively straightforward for the DfES to commit to funding both schemes. These arrangements applied only to English universities since, under the devolution arrangements for Scotland and Wales, higher education was a matter for the devolved administrations (Northern Ireland had its own arrangements). The policy consistently applied, and subsequently maintained by the Conservative/Liberal Democrat coalition government, was to devolve responsibility away from the centre. The Department for Innovation, Universities and Skills (DIUS)[17] was therefore determined to delegate the administration of the new schemes since, in addition to the financial goals of the policy, the aim also was to increase responsibilities and hence the autonomy of HE institutions.

Implementation of the schemes was preceded by a consultation period with universities. An advisory group on voluntary giving, composed of representatives from universities and further education colleges, Universities UK, the Higher Education Funding Council for England (HEFCE), CASE Europe and the Ross Group, helped to design the details of the scheme.

The start-up scheme 2005-08

Under the scheme the Department for Education and Skills committed £7.5m over the three years 2005-08 to help universities build up their fundraising capacity. This was straightforward budgetary support on a 50/50 basis. The purpose was to increase the number of institutions who were forming fundraising teams by reducing risk and the costs to a university of investing in fundraising for the first time. The latent interest in the HE sector was at once apparent, when some seventy applications were received.

To evaluate so many applications represented quite a heavy administrative burden. Consonant with the policy of devolving where possible, the

---

[17] The DIUS, formed in 2007, took over some of the functions of the DfES before merging with the Department of Trade and Industry in 2009 to form the Department for Business, Innovation and Skills (BIS).

Department, with difficulty, persuaded UUK to undertake the administration of the start-up scheme. It says a good deal about the slow pace of change that as late as 2005 the professional body representing all higher education bodies in the UK did not think that playing a role in the development of university fundraising was part of their remit. Their reluctance reflected this lack of policy commitment, and thus the absence of interest, expertise or knowledge of the growing university fundraising sector. Consequently the staff of UUK had no experience in fundraising or in the number and nature of staff required to implement a policy of fundraising. It was therefore not surprising that they lacked the confidence to take on the responsibility of judging between the applications received, and to run a process that would be seen to be fair by the very disparate constituents represented within UUK[18].

Here again the work of CASE Europe and the individuals who had started the professionalisation of university fundraising proved its worth, since UUK were able to turn to the pool of university development directors – fully experienced in the day to day work of running a fundraising operation in an academic environment – to run the selection process. The group was chaired by Dr Mary Blair, the development director at LSE, who had served as a member of the government task force which produced the Thomas Report. All applications were then scored by at least two serving development directors, and the group then made recommendations to a subcommittee of vice-chancellors from UUK, who vetted and approved the recommendations virtually unchanged.[19] As a result, twenty-seven institutions received three-year grants of 50 per cent of their new fundraising costs (mostly staff positions and start-up equipment). By thus reducing the financial costs of investing in the start-up fundraising operations, the government also reduced the internal 'political' risks run by universities in initiating a new non-academic activity whose success in each individual case still had to be proved.

Important though this financial support was, the benefits of the scheme depended on developing greater understanding at the institutional level of what was required for a successful fundraising policy. The need to engage a much wider range of people in the higher education sector – vice-chancellors, chairmen

---

[18]   Conversation of the author with Ruth Thompson, Director, then Director General, Higher Education, DoES, 2003-09.
[19]   Author's conversation with Dr Mary Blair, 10 April 2012.

of governing bodies, academics, deans – was evident. There was also a shortage of staff with relevant skills, hence the need for professional training for development staff. So in support of capacity building, the DfES made a further grant of £2 million to fund CASE training programmes. As well as helping the growing need for development staff, these programmes over time included professional staff at all levels and in all areas – finance and administrative staff, as well as fundraising staff. A new and important component of the programmes were special small group training events for vice-chancellors, governors and academics to convey the fundamental point that a range of leaders within an institution had a role to play in fundraising. By 2012, nearly ten years later, all twenty-seven universities which received start-up grants continued to fundraise and were raising sufficient sums in the context of their own budgets for each institution to maintain and expand its fundraising activities.

Matched funding scheme for donations 2008-2011

Having launched the start-up scheme, the DfES and HEFCE moved on to the broader scheme to encourage all universities in England to recruit new donors. However, capacity building through the start-up scheme had to come first and be given time to produce results, so that those universities new to fundraising (mostly former polytechnics) had a fair chance of benefiting.

As a result there was a time-lag between the start of the two schemes, which meant that there was an attractive pot of money in the education budget which a succession of ministers with innovative ideas in the educational field were sometimes tempted to raid. However, there was much at stake in continuing to ring-fence these resources to support fundraising, since the policy could take time to show results. Fortunately, senior ministers understood what was at stake, preserving the set aside fund until the launch of the matched funding scheme three years later.

To emphasise the importance of the scheme, a public announcement was issued by the Prime Minister, Tony Blair, in February 2007. This set out the government's intention to allocate £200 million over three years to match donations received from new donors. The idea was to incentivise all universities to recruit new sources of financial support. Details of the scheme had to be worked out so that existing successful fundraising operations did not scoop the pool. Universities were able to choose between three tiers in which gifts were matched in a different ratio but with different caps suitable for institutions with differing degrees of fundraising experience. Again, the aim was to spread the funds as widely as possible across the sector.

In announcing the scheme the prime minister referred to the arguments over the introduction of higher fees in 1998 and 2006 as a move to get more money into the higher education sector:

> Our critics said tuition fees would harm participation. But the figures yesterday showed that student applications are not only rising again, but that they are at their highest ever level. However, it is important that our universities have every opportunity to raise the resources they need.

That's why this fundraising plan is so important. It will incentivise all universities to raise more charitable and private funding. Increasing voluntary giving is a vital step in enabling institutions to build up substantial giving over the longer term[20]

It was now recognised by the prime minister himself that university fundraising was a national priority, thus crowning some twenty years later the timid encouragement of fundraising by the Conference of University Administrators.[21] Despite the vagaries of politics and the global economic crisis, which transformed national finances from 2008, both Gordon Brown, Tony Blair's successor as prime minister, and the Conservative/Liberal Democratic coalition government, which took office in 2010, have stayed with the policy.

The financial results speak for themselves. No fewer than 135 higher education institutions took part in the matched funding scheme. They raised some £580 million over the three years of the scheme, attracting extra funds of over £140 million from HEFCE.[22] In addition, the objective of broadening the fundraising effort by increasing the number of HE institutions in which fundraising was a

---

[20]   DfES press release of Prime Minister's announcement, 16 February 2007.
[21]   CUA Report, op. cit. (See Chapter 3 above).
[22]   HEFCE (2012) Statement of 2 February 2012 *Voluntary giving to higher education : success and challenges for the next decade.* [online] http://www.hefce.ac.uk/.

regular activity had been substantially achieved. By 2011 some 160 institutions out of the 170 HE institutions in England and Wales (as well as universities in Scotland and Northern Ireland which are outside the HEFCE remit) were actively engaged in raising funds from private donors – a remarkable achievement in the short time since the Thomas Report of 2004. Moreover, it was a condition of participation in the matched funding scheme that those taking part should submit data to the Ross-CASE annual survey of gift revenue and fundraising costs. So participation in the scheme greatly improved the breadth and quality of the data in the survey, which remains the only source of such valuable data.

The official view of the scheme's results was that it had generated 'a major increase in philanthropic giving to our universities and colleges. It has also created a step change in the approach to fundraising and the skills needed.'[23] To maintain momentum HEFCE decided some independent evaluation of the progress made and the way ahead was required. HEFCE accordingly set up a review committee in early 2012 chaired by a serving vice-chancellor, Professor Shirley Pearce[24], of Loughborough University.

The Pearce Review[25]

There had been major changes in the environment for fundraising in higher education institutions since the 2003 White Paper. In addition to the deterioration in the global and national economic climate which affected governments and individuals alike, there were particular changes in the UK – notably the increase in student fees. With the conclusion of the matched funding scheme for donations in August 2011, HEFCE therefore commissioned an independent review of the results of the scheme, with terms of reference to evaluate progress made in the last decade and identify challenges to be addressed, if progress was to continue.

---

[23] Sir Alan Langlands, HEFCE Chief Executive, in HEFCE statement, op. cit.
[24] Other members were Nick Blinco, Director of Development and Alumni Relations, University of Birmingham; Rory Brooks, MML Capital Partners LLP; Professor Sir Richard Trainor, King's College London and Martin Williams, Department for Business Innovation and Skills.
[25] Report to HEFCE (2012) Review of Philanthropy in UK Higher Education September 2012 [online] http://www.hefce.ac.uk/. (The Pearce Review).

The review noted the 'remarkable results' universities had achieved by their increased investment in fundraising. The national picture over a longer time frame supported this positive conclusion. In 2004-05 the seventy-five institutions taking part in the Ross/CASE survey reported raising £350 million in philanthropic gifts (with an estimated additional £100 million raised by institutions not participating in the survey); alumni donors were an estimated 90,000. In 2006-07, 131 institutions reported funds raised as £513 million from 132,000 donors. 'Five years later this had risen to 152 institutions reporting £693 million from 204,000 donors – 16% more institutions reporting an annual rise of 35% in funds raised and 54% more donors."[26] It confirmed that the results achieved over the past ten years showed that policy was now on the right lines.

The review emphasised that these positive results had been achieved by a range of universities, many of whom were investing in fundraising for the first time. Looking to the future it accepted that its recommendations for further government action – a repeat of the successful 'matching' scheme for donations, and the suggestions for tax reforms to encourage charitable giving – were unlikely to be implemented in current economic circumstances. These and the recommendations for action by universities – greater involvement of lay leadership, encouragement for academics to play a part, better professional training for staff – helped to consolidate messages from the seminal Thomas Report of 2004.

On the cautionary side, noting the important role played by alumni giving, the review warned that the 'student experience' once in residence was critical to alumni attitudes when considering a gift to their old university in later life. The US experience after fifty years of consistent fundraising was that 'the participation rate in the US from alumni of public universities is circa 10%'[27]. Since the current alumni participation rate in the UK was estimated at 1.2 per cent, the review suggested that a target of 5 per cent participation rate for the UK sector by 2022 might be realistic.[28] A more immediate warning was the need to expand the workforce of trained professionals. Professor Shirley Pearce saw this as the major bottleneck to an expansion of university fundraising.

---

[26]   Pearce Review, op. cit., p. 16, para 22 and Ross/CASE survey 2010-11 table 3.18.
[27]   Pearce Review, op. cit., p. 62, para 174.
[28]   Ibid.

The review contained eloquent passages on the importance of philanthropy, the role of fundraising and the benefits which flow from successful programmes, while showing there was some way to go before fundraising took its place as a core activity of every university. Overall the impression left was that the target readership still had to be persuaded to persevere in this new effort: 'Universities must hold their nerve [...] if they do, they have the opportunity to receive £2 billion per annum [...] by 2022.'[29]

The Pearce Review and other official comments cited above thus give a generally optimistic picture of the opportunities for university fundraising. It remains to be seen whether, in the context of general economic austerity and higher fees in English and Welsh universities, levels of alumni giving will be maintained and increased, as the review believes is possible.

The review concentrates on the need for universities to develop an 'asking' culture and a more professional approach to fundraising. It was not asked to deal with the other side of the equation, namely the motivation of donors, to help evaluate whether this hopeful picture of the role of philanthropy in support of British higher education is justified. Some account of the position from the donor's point of view is therefore necessary.

---

[29] Ibid., foreword, p.3, para 8 and p. 62, para 173.

8

Philanthropy and fundraising: a moral maze?

'The purest treasure mortal times afford
Is spotless reputation.'[1]

Who gives and why?

Classical anthropologists have written at length about the role of gifts and counter gifts in non-industrialised societies. One authority concludes that 'the social relations set up by gift exchange are among the most powerful forces which bind society together'[2]. A duty of giving for charitable purposes is recognised in all the major religions. An obligation to give for the relief of poverty and other pious acts is one of the five pillars of Islam; it is incumbent on all Buddhists to 'make merit' by giving alms to local temples or gifts of food to young monks who daily circulate with their begging bowls. There are similar injunctions in the Old and New Testaments.

By definition, a philanthropic gift is altruistic. Yet psychologists and social scientists suggest that there is invariably a mixture of motives in a decision to give – even on the part of voluntary donors to the National Blood Transfusion Service where neither donor nor recipient know each other's identity. Among the range of motives for giving, besides altruism, some most often cited are gratitude, reciprocity, social prestige, guilt, shame, penance and bribery. European universities from their mediaeval origins have benefited from this

---

[1]   Richard II, Act I, Scene i.
[2]   Titmus, R. M. (1979) *The Gift Relationship*. London: Allen and Unwin. p. 73

universal human propensity to give. Their early growth has been described as 'institutional responses to the need to harness the expanding intellectual forces of the eleventh and twelfth centuries to the ecclesiastical, governmental and professional requirements of society [...]Their essential purpose had been to augment the number of trained personnel to meet the demands of secular authorities, the Church and the organised professions.'[3]

In this early period the notion of a university in Northern Europe was seen as 'in essence, a masters' guild run by and for the benefit of its members and their associated students'[4]. The English universities were not wealthy: 'during the elaborate building operations of the fifteenth century, their finances were strained to the point where much recourse had to be made to private donations'.[5] The reliance of mediaeval universities on private donations, as well as on funding from church and state, is paralleled in modern times. Most, if not all, the great civic universities of the nineteenth and early twentieth century were financed initially by local philanthropists, through gifts of land and buildings as well as cash, and by public subscription from many levels of society. The University of Sheffield was founded in part 'by penny donations made by working people in the city'[6]. So civic pride and respect for learning can perhaps be added to the mediaeval motives listed above.

In the contemporary world the sentiments expressed by some of the 105 billionaires who have signed The Giving Pledge, launched publicly by Bill Gates and Warren Buffet in 2010, might be added to the universal human motives for giving discussed above. This pledge 'is a commitment by the world's wealthiest individuals and families to dedicate the majority of their wealth to philanthropy'.[7] By March 2012 over a hundred dollar billionaires had signed, giving in total pledges worth over $125 billion based on a conservative estimate of aggregate wealth. In the individual responses explaining their decisions to give, a number of themes come through – the wish 'to give something back', the desire to make a difference, the pleasure and 'deep fulfilment' of philanthropic acts.

---

[3] Cobban, A.B. (1988) The Medieval English Universities. Aldershot: Scholar Press. p. 10.

[4] Ibid., p.109.

[5] Ibid., p.110.

[6] Professor K Barnett, Vice-Chancellor, University of Sheffield, cited in the 11th issue (2010) of the University's Donor News, p. 3.

[7] See official website at www.givingpledge.org.

Another theme, articulated by Bill Gates, but reflected in many other comments was 'how to make philanthropy as impactful as possible'.[8] Since education and medical research are frequent categories which attract philanthropic support there are lessons here for universities, the most successful of which take pains in matching their donors to university priorities and engaging with them at a policy level. The notion of impactful giving has also resulted in universities developing events and ceremonies to involve the donor community in an interesting and enjoyable way. When engaging in major fundraising programmes, universities have sought to provide the right environment for donors at all levels whilst bearing in mind the danger to academic independence of outside interference.

Aside from these general considerations on donor motivation there is one aspect of philanthropy specific to universities, namely alumni giving, where one key motivation in the US and the UK differs. In both British and American universities alumni giving is invariably prompted by a mixture of motives, of which the dominant one is the wish 'to give something back' mentioned above by many of the billionaire signatories to the Giving Pledge. In US universities this is often combined with 'legacy' giving (in a metaphorical sense, meaning a desire to develop a relationship which will help in the university admissions procedure for the donor's children or near relatives). In the United States this is still a key motivation because, despite the high level of tuition fees, competition for places is fierce. In the moral and political climate of the UK the idea is anathema that wealth or personal connections could affect the decision to admit a student.

Academic Concerns

The utilitarian role of the mediaeval universities and their reliance in part on private donations for their development echo modern controversies over academic freedom and sources of funding, in particular over the extent to which universities should be responsive to externally defined objectives in determining their research and teaching programmes. In modern times, the main concerns within the academic community relate first to the risk of a conflict of interest between an external funder and a scholar or scientist freely pursuing a line of

---

[8]   http://blogs.marketwatch.com/thetell/2012/09/18/more-billionaire-families-join-buffett-and-gates-philanthropy-effort/.

teaching or research; and second to a reputational risk in public perceptions of a given transaction. These concerns can arise not only in the case of philanthropic donations from private individuals, foundations or companies, but equally from financial support in the form of research grants or contract research, where deliverables are required on a given timescale, whether commercially sponsored or government-funded.

More substantively, there are fears that some categories of donor – companies or other vested interests or a strong minded individual philanthropist – will attach conditions to a gift that compromise the independence of scholarly or scientific work. It is clearly the duty of the individual, the research group or the central university authority, when negotiating financial support, to seek a shared objective with a donor and to ensure that inappropriate conditions are ruled out, or the support declined.

Fears of improper influence are not confined to private financial support: it can also cause difficulties even with public funding sources.[9] The excesses of totalitarian states, such as Stalin's well-known decision in favour of TD Lysenko's school of genetics (with disastrous results for Soviet agriculture[10]), can be left out of the discussion. At the other end of the spectrum the British government aroused grave disquiet in the UK scientific community by the proposal made in a Green Paper in 1971 that part of the budgets of the government funded research councils devoted to applied research should be allocated on a customer-contractor basis.[11] Despite the distinction made between 'basic' and 'applied' research, this was seen as an attack on the freedom of the academic to pursue objective, independent lines of enquiry, scholarly or scientific.

---

[9]   See for example the LSE academic who said that once upon a time 'academics wouldn't even accept money from the Ministry of Defence', quoted in the Woolf Report, Chapter 3, Section V, Subsection B, para 3.186.

[10]   Schapiro, L (1962) The Communist Party of the Soviet Union. London: Eyre + Spottiswoode. p. 531. For another agricultural example in the USSR – how to enhance to productivity of the Ukrainian grasslands – see Khruschev, N (1974) *Khruschev Remembers*. Translated and edited by Talbot, S. Boston: Little Brown & Co.

[11]   Government Green Paper. (1971) *A Framework for Government Research and Development*. Cmnd 4814. London: HMSO.

The author of the proposals in the Green Paper was not some uncivilised apparatchik but a Fellow of the Royal Society, an honorary fellow of Trinity College, Cambridge, and the head of the government's Central Policy Review Staff, Lord (Victor) Rothschild. He recalled wryly that 'no less than 121 scientists and/or doctors signed letters of protest to *The Times*'.[12] Lord Rothschild went on to discuss in public lectures and speeches the uproar his ideas had caused.[13]

Thus tensions can arise whatever the source of funding – government, charitable foundation, corporate or individual. Universities draw a clear distinction between philanthropic donations and contract research. Contract research grants have clear deliverables over an agreed time frame for a particular piece of research whereas philanthropic gifts are made with no expectation of material reward. Academics in UK universities are nowadays more familiar with the need to submit project proposals to a wide variety of sources and to agree objectives with their sponsors. Lord Rothschild would have the satisfaction of knowing that today, some forty years later, his approach is generally understood and accepted.

Despite the hazards it could be argued that universities, given their charitable status, have a duty to fundraise, and thus to maximise their income. There is no body of opinion arguing in principle against the acceptance of outside donations, but there are those who oppose the organised solicitation of gifts, though it is not clear what their preferred alternative would be. These few voices criticising the rise of organised fundraising by universities rely on a mixture of moral and practical arguments. The practical arguments usually categorise the current model of fundraising, as discussed in earlier chapters, as overly influenced by American practice (and therefore by definition unseemly?), insensitive to local conditions and too bureaucratic and expensive.

What follows focuses on the moral arguments regarding 'philanthropic' fundraising, though the risks involved and the principles to be followed are broadly the same for philanthropic and for 'contract' type financial support.

---

[12] Rothschild, Lord (1977) *Meditations of a Broomstick*. London: Collins St James Place, p.68.
[13] Ibid., Chapters 8 and 9.

Reputational risk: the source of funds

If financial support from governments can give rise to problems, universities have to be equally aware of the reputational risk arising from the character of individual donors or the source of the wealth from which the donation is made.

Vetting the source of philanthropic funds is not a simple matter. If individuals have made their fortunes in industry, is it necessary to investigate conditions in their factories to ensure that profits were ethically earned (e.g. no child labour)? If so, what level of donation should attract detailed investigation? If the individual is dead, but has left a philanthropic foundation, do the same considerations apply? Should the business careers of a Carnegie or Mellon or Rockefeller be investigated before applying for grants from the distinguished foundations they established? There is also the argument that 'bad' money is a subjective concept, and in any case can still do good, so a donation from a 'tainted' source should still be considered rather than automatically rejected.[14]

The responsibility for answering such questions and for decisions on the acceptance of a gift rests with the governing body concerned. Whilst common sense is initially as good a guide as any, with the expansion of fundraising some governing bodies have developed published guidelines and more formal procedures for vetting a proposed gift.

An institutional code of ethics

As early as 1982 CASE as an organisation developed a statement of ethics to govern the professional standards of fundraising in the education sector.[15] In 2005 the Council for Industry and Education, in conjunction with the Institute of Business Ethics, published a report on the situation in UK universities which

---

[14]   A well-known example, though not in a university context, was *Encounter*, a leading literary magazine founded in 1953 by Stephen Spender, who resigned in 1967 on discovering that the magazine was funded by the CIA and not American philanthropists.

[15]   Text at www.case.org, adopted in Toronto, July 1982.

found 'no coherent or consistent approach to documenting ethical policy'.[16] More recently, CASE Europe and a group of UK development directors have published guidelines for the acceptance of gifts.[17]

The growing recognition of the importance of ethical guidelines and clear institution-wide procedures was given renewed impetus by the publication of the Woolf Report[18], an inquiry set up by the council of the London School of Economics, into the School's links with Libya. The issues raised went well beyond fundraising and dealt with a range of academic activities which cumulatively bore on the School's reputation. They were of sufficient importance that when the Report was received the School's director considered it his duty to resign.

The details of the links, encouraged by the British government, do not concern us here. What is important is that the links developed in such a way that 'the LSE had effectively tied part of its reputation to that of Libya, and more particularly to Saif Gaddafi'.[19] The report describes how the relationship developed in a piecemeal fashion such that there was no overall picture of the various Libyan links with departments which had grown up over the years. As a result the School did not, and was not in a position to, conduct a due diligence assessment which any global company would undertake before embarking on a relationship with a foreign partner.[20]

Lord Woolf's conclusion was that the university should so organise itself that an overview of the activities of the constituent departments, which could have repercussions on a university's work and reputation, is readily available.

In the narrower context of fundraising, Lord Woolf raised four questions of general relevance:

---

[16]   Brunel University and Council for Industry and Higher Education (CIHE) (2005) Ethics Matters: Managing Ethical Issues in Higher Education. London: CIHE, p.7.

[17]   CASE (2011) CASE Europe: Ethical Principles behind the Acceptance of Gifts – Guidelines for Higher Education Institutions. Developed with the Ross and 1994 Group of Development Directors. [online] http://www.case.org/.

[18]   LSE Report (2011) An Inquiry into the LSE's links with Libya and Lessons to be Learned (October 2011). [online] http://www.woolflse.com/ (Woolf Report).

[19]   Woolf Report, ibid., para 1.3. Saif was the son of Colonel Gaddafi.

[20]   Ibid., para 1.13.

i)   Should individual members of the academic staff solicit donations for the institution independently of any central guidance?

ii) If a donation comes from a foundation, is it necessary to look behind the legal entity and into the sources of its funds?

iii) Who should be responsible for deciding to accept or reject a controversial donation? What information do they need to make that decision? Who should be responsible for giving it to them?

iv) If a donation is accepted, what limits should there be on the donor's involvement in the use of the funds? What amounts to an unacceptable conflict of interest between a donor and a recipient of the donation?[21]

Lord Woolf's prime conclusion was that the LSE should 'have an embedded code dealing with reputational risk which applies across the institution'.[22] It will be readily apparent that this analysis goes well beyond fundraising questions, and raises wider issues of management and policy control. Moreover, the sheer size of modern universities means that what could once be dealt with on the basis of common sense and trust now requires a more formal approach. Indeed the need for accepted procedures for reputational risk assessment across an institution is now increasingly accepted.

Although arising from the specific circumstances of one distinguished higher education institution, other universities will recognise elements of this analysis as relevant to their circumstances too. These issues have arisen from the unprecedented expansion of British higher education and the need for the best institutions to maintain the quality of their teaching and research at international standards if they are to remain competitive at the global level.

---

[21]   Woolf Report, ibid., para 1.20.
[22]   Woolf Report, ibid., recommendation 1, p.142.

9
Future outlook

Given the spread of professional fundraising across the UK higher education sector, it is timely to consider what the risks and opportunities for fundraising really are and whether the official optimism expressed in the Pearce Review is justified.[1] In the last two or three generations the university sector has expanded out of all recognition. So much so that a 2013 report of the Office for National Statistics noted that '47 per cent of those who completed a degree in the past five years were working in roles such as sales assistants and care workers [...] up from 39 per cent in 2008'.[2] A subsequent leading article commented 'Public policy needs to avoid promoting fruitless study [...] young people's horizons will not be widened by pushing university for its own sake.'[3] A university education, admittedly with an expanded definition, is now the common experience of nearly half the population. If many young graduates continue to face reduced employment prospects there may be a less positive context for fundraising than the Pearce Review envisaged.

The higher education sector is no longer a small group of relatively homogenous institutions; despite political pressure to maintain a notional equality, there is now a range of universities which vary in mission, quality – and price. In addition, many have a global role, whether in student recruitment, attracting academic talent, or working to international standards of research, and sometimes even in geographical presence.

The growth of fundraising has to be seen in the context of these great changes. What was often done, if done at all, on an informal basis by individuals, now

---

[1]   See Chapter 7.

[2]   Groom, B. (2013) 'Half of university leavers settle for lower pay'. *Financial Times*. 20 November 2013. p.3.

[3]   Editorial. (2013) 'Aiming Higher'. *Financial Times*. 25 November 2013. p. 12.

requires professional staff, the involvement of powerful personalities outside the university and more time from the top university leadership. And this in a period when the sheer size of universities, the variety of the student body, the complexity of the research base and the weight of government regulations, has added immeasurably to the administrative load. Against such a background the fundraising function has to marshal its case for a share of the budget and leadership time, both lay and academic.

When university fundraising is looked at in the context of the wider charitable sector, the results achieved by the universities under the various government schemes of the past five to ten years are encouraging. Although only a handful of UK billionaires have signed up for the Giving Pledge donations to the UK charitable sector remains substantial. In 2011-12 the Charities Aid Foundation and the National Council for Voluntary Organisations jointly reported total gifts for the year as £9.3 billion though this in real terms was the smallest since records began in 2004-05. [4]

In the university sector for the same year, although the government's matched funding scheme had ended, overall year on year growth continued. The annual Ross/CASE survey for 2011-12 reported total funds raised as £774 million, a 14 per cent increase over the previous year. The number of donors also increased to 214,000 (up from 204,000).[5] The result is a growing recognition by university leaders that there is a strong correlation between fundraising success and the size of investment and the longevity of fundraising programmes. In turn this has led to a growing understanding that the right answer to a failing programme is not to terminate it, but to analyse the causes of failure and remedy them.[6] The success of a wide range of institutions in securing substantial returns on their investment in fundraising has led to a change of attitude whereby fundraising has become a normal and acceptable activity for a university to undertake. There is, however, little material on those universities who have initiated a fundraising programme and stopped it. An analysis of such cases could provide useful pointers to what went wrong and what is needed to turn failure into success.

---

[4]   UK Giving 2012 at www.cafonline.org.
[5]   Ross/CASE Report 2011/12. [online] http://www.philanthropy-impact.org/.
[6]   See discussion in the Pearce Review, op. cit., Appendix 4, p.97 et seq.

More generally the Pearce Review identified two major issues for the future: the availability of professional staff, and the need for a university's leadership to persevere in an active fundraising policy. To take the practical issue of staffing first: the role of CASE and CASE Europe, as has been shown in previous chapters, has been critical in developing professional standards and in training at all levels. Yet lack of trained staff remains a bottleneck. Staff shortages, particularly at senior level, can lead both to bidding up salary levels in a competitive situation, and to premature job-hopping. A measure of continuity in professional leadership is important for success both in winning the confidence of the academic community and in providing direction and impetus to the professional staff. No doubt this trend will continue to be a difficulty as more universities expand their operations, and so they will continue to need CASE Europe and to explore other sources of training, including in-house training and online courses.

Unhappily the shortage of trained personnel is particularly acute at the senior level. This deficiency highlights the link between staffing issues and the commitment of universities to persevere in their fundraising tasks, as recommended in the Pearce Review. An expansion in fundraising requires a decision on the part of the university leadership to increase the investment. At a time of severe economic pressures this is a difficult decision to make and have accepted by the academic community. The ability of professional staff to win the confidence of the academic community is critical to the whole policy. Building academic confidence requires leadership, a long term approach, continuity in staffing, ability to build a team, senior management skills and minimum ego. Not all these qualities are readily acquired on training courses.

A fundraiser's credibility with academics is thus fundamental to success. Building trust between fundraisers and the academic community is a topic not sufficiently dealt with in training courses. It is not a one-way street, and the academic community too needs a greater understanding of what the fundraising process entails. By and large today most academics accept that universities need to fundraise, and that fundraising can succeed in UK circumstances. There are disagreements on how to go about it, and friction arises when fundraisers are thought to claim credit for what academics have done, or for donations 'which would have come in anyway'.

This is to misunderstand the role of fundraisers – indeed the term itself is a misnomer since fundraisers are only part of the fundraising process. Their role in essence is to support the academic in striking the spark of interest in the mind of a potential benefactor. They are there to look after the planning and logistics of meetings and to bring a donor to the point of decision, to arrange the necessary follow-up, and back office work. These necessary and mostly unglamorous tasks do not compete with but complement and support the role of academics. While home-grown talent is on the increase (and perhaps more academics will find their way into the profession), some universities which recruit academic staff and students on a global basis may need to do the same with non-academic staff, including fundraisers.

Other fundraising issues for the future arise from the growth of the student body. Many more families are implicated and therefore interested in the state of our universities, suggesting that new programmes are needed to involve parents and grandparents. Universities with clinical schools, or with research departments linked to major hospitals, have done particularly well in fundraising.[7] It may be that synergies will develop between such universities and hospitals in instituting new fundraising programmes, including 'grateful patient' programmes which have hitherto been outside the comfort zone of most hospitals in the UK.

As the 2011-12 Ross/CASE survey[8] of fundraising makes clear, universities vary in the maturity and effectiveness of their fundraising. The generally positive progress cannot be expected to be uniform across the sector. As can be seen from that survey, 39 per cent of institutions saw a increase in new funds secured and 31 per cent reported an increase in cash income. However, 27 per cent of institutions saw their new funds secured drop by over 50 per cent.

Nevertheless, the human propensity to give is deep-rooted and universal. Higher education in the UK for too long neglected the opportunities. Universities, in presenting their case for support to ever widening constituencies at home and abroad, have left the supposed 'ivory tower'

---

[7] Pearce Review, ibid., Appendix 4, p.98.

[8] Ross/CASE Report 2011/12 op. cit.

deplored by their critics. They are increasingly involved with the societies affected by their teaching and research programmes, the world from which their students come, and the workplaces to which they go. The risks are evident, but as the Pearce Review made clear, so are the opportunities.

PART II

Fundraising at
Oxford and Cambridge:
a personal view

Oxford's Big Bang

In 1988 the University of Oxford announced the opening of the Campaign for Oxford with an initial target of £220 million. This courageous move – breaking the academic taboos about inviting Mammon into academe, and relieving government of its near total responsibility for higher education – had a profound effect on academic opinion nationally. In one move it rendered fundraising for higher education respectable, and gave new hope to those struggling to build an effective operation in universities across the country.

The architect of this policy was Sir Patrick (now Lord) Neill, a former warden of All Souls, and at the time vice-chancellor of the university. Tall and austere, a distinguished lawyer and public servant, he was the ultimate 'establishment' figure, and the last person one would expect to see leading a fundraising campaign. Whether or not he found the whole business distasteful, he was convinced of the need for Oxford to seek additional sources of revenue from the private sector and put the force of his personality into convincing first his immediate colleagues, and then the Oxford academic community at large, through open debate in Congregation, the university's academic parliament.

This first campaign for Oxford was far and away the largest university fundraising target to date and light years away from the 'appeal targets' recorded in the CUA report in 1984.[1]

Oxford had shared the general academic malaise of the early eighties brought on by restrictions in government funding. At the time the campaign was announced, some ninety academic posts had been left vacant for lack of funds, investment in infrastructure had virtually ceased and academic opinion was seriously concerned that Oxford would lose its capacity to compete for talent

---

[1]　See Part I, Chapter 3 above.

worldwide, and thus be unable to maintain its international reputation. It has to be said that financial management at Oxford had not been as tight as it might have been, so that by the middle of the decade there was a general recognition among the academics that a financial crisis was in the offing. Thus the academic community was prepared for drastic measures to restore the situation.

In the early 1980s Sir Patrick Neill, who was vice-chancellor elect at the time (1983-85), was convinced of the need to secure new sources of finance for the university. [2] The then vice-chancellor was reputedly not keen to get involved with fundraising himself, so Sir Patrick 'spent much time talking about money to people within the university, colleges and connected outsiders (alumni etc). I had realized that the university needed money in order to do all the things that needed to be done. I also knew that it was not possible to get this money from the State. I spent a good deal of my two years as vice-chancellor elect planning how we might organise a campaign'.

Having got to know Nicholas Ulanov, then working for McKinsey, Sir Patrick persuaded the University to authorise the consultants to do a report on fundraising by Oxford, its feasibility and the right way to go about it. Their report backed the idea of the university running a fundraising campaign.

Apart from the intrinsic difficulties of successfully implementing an active fundraising policy, there were internal problems too. Besides cultural argument against fundraising ('Oxford does not do that sort of thing'), perhaps the greatest difficulty those arguing for the new policy had to face was that many colleges were already running their own campaigns for the benefit of themselves and did not feel attracted by the idea of supporting a campaign run by the university. It was thought that the loyalty of old members was to their colleges rather than to the university. Some of the greatest opponents were senior heads of house and it took some time to the change their minds. Even so the tactical conflict of interest as to who should approach a given alumnus/a, college or university, caused difficulties once the Campaign for Oxford got under way:

---

[2]   The following quotations are taken from a communication from Lord Neill to the author of 26 February 2014.

Eventually a truce was agreed whereby together the college concerned and the university would work out which institution would be more likely to success in obtaining a donation. It was an uneasy truce.

The university adopted the McKinsey five-year plan which included fundraising offices in New York and Tokyo besides the main office in Oxford, and came with a fully costed multimillion pound budget. Initially Sir Patrick had in mind a target of £30 million, but after consulting Oxonians on both sides of the Atlantic, this was raised to £220 million. If the proposed campaign was to be taken seriously by major philanthropic foundations, the size of the target had to be such as would have a significant effect on Oxford's finances.

The academic community had to be committed to the enterprise, because of the resource implications of staffing up a professional fundraising office on a scale to meet such a large target. To avoid repetitious debates and challenges to an annual budget, Sir Patrick took the risk in 1987 of presenting a five year plan and budget for debate by Congregation. Despite the college difficulties mentioned above, he won the approval of the academic community and the action shifted to implementation. He now had to make good his conviction that Oxford was capable of raising these unprecedented sums.

To lead the fundraising team, Dr Henry Drucker was recruited from the University of Edinburgh where he had been one of a group of younger academics supervising the small development office (see Chapter 3 above). As an American, an academic and with some experience of fundraising in a UK university environment, his was a rare combination of attributes and a highly credible appointment. With his jaunty manner , he was the antithesis of the vice-chancellor. But the passion and the belief he brought to his work matched Sir Patrick's own convictions. 'However ill matched they appeared, they made a formidable team.'[3] The Campaign for Oxford was formally opened in a splendid university ceremony in the Sheldonian Theatre. A special train (only first-class carriages, and with refreshments) brought journalists and other guests from London to take part in the festivities, and to raise the profile of this new policy.

---

[3]   Author's conversation with Anne Lonsdale, formerly Director of External Relations Office, University of Oxford.

This got the Campaign for Oxford off to a good start and by 1993 the official campaign total raised was £340 million (including research grants and contracts).

The Cambridge Case, or Little by Little

The situation in Cambridge

In the decades leading up to World War One there was an increasing need for investment in staff and infrastructure to sustain the growth in 'new' subjects (often based on professorships established much earlier) such as physics, chemistry, physiology and engineering. The period 1870-1914 has been described as the 'most remarkable [of the] high points in university building [...] the (more so) since it came at a time when resources were extremely limited, and without government aid.'[4] The period began with a benefaction from the seventh Duke of Devonshire, chancellor of the university, to build the Cavendish Laboratory (the university's department of physics). Occasional gifts, even on this scale, did not meet the increasing financial needs. In 1898 at the suggestion of the vice-chancellor (Alexander Hill, Master of Downing College) the university decided to form a new group - the Cambridge University Association (CUA) - from members and friends of the university 'whose primary object shall be to procure the better endowment of the University as a place of education, religion, learning, and research'.[5] The inaugural meeting was held at Devonshire House in London on 1 February 1899 and chaired by the eighth Duke of Devonshire, who had succeeded his father as chancellor of the university. In opening the meeting the chancellor set out the issue: 'there is a general and traditional belief that the University of Cambridge is in possession [...] of ample endowments sufficient to enable it to carry on in a satisfactory manner the great and important work that it does in the nation - that whereas this traditional belief exists, no conclusion could be possibly more remote from the actual fact'. Reflecting the general ignorance of the university's internal

---

[4]   Brooke, N.L. (1993) *A History of the University of Cambridge, Vol IV 1870-1990.* Cambridge: Cambridge University Press.

[5]   Clark, J.W. (1904) *Endowments of the University of Cambridge* (Cam.c.1.23.7). Cambridge: Cambridge University Press, p. 597.

affairs Lord Rothschild remarked that 'During the happy years I spent at Cambridge I do not know that either I myself, or my fellow undergraduates, ever thought anything of the revenues of our University. If we did, we thought she was fully endowed, and any deficit there was might be made up by the fines that were often levied on us.' Two of the academics present then gave examples of the need. The regius professor of physic[6], Clifford Allbut, explained how 'the General Board of Studies was asked to make the appointment of a lecturer [...] and the man was found. For two or three years he did the teaching, but the General Board could not find him any pay.'

In turn Alfred Ewing, professor of mechanism and applied mechanics, recounted his efforts to fund a building to teach engineering. 'No funds were available from which we might establish an engineering laboratory. It was impossible to ask for more than a site. We got that, and after waiting for a little time for the millionaire who did not come – we made an appeal to the public.'[7] As a result of pledges made at this meeting and subsequently the CUA had raised £71,799 by 1904. The list of subscribers and the individual sums donated was published, and was led by the chancellor, N.M. Rothschild and Sons (Lord Rothschild) and W.W. Astor, who each gave £10,000.[8] Fundraising by the CUA continued intermittently into the 1920s, but by the end of World War II the association was moribund. In 1951 the council of senate adjourned any discussion of its re-establishment; the accounts for 1952 showed an income of £27 against expenses of £30; and in 1953 the council decided to take over the administration of the remaining funds.[9] The association, despite the inglorious end of its activities, had set a valuable precedent for cooperation between academics and powerful well-wishers outside the university.

By the 1980s, after two world wars and several generations of students and academics almost entirely funded by the taxpayer, the generality of academics

---

[6]   The formal term for the head of the Clinical School of Medicine.
[7]   These quotations were copied verbatim by the author from the printed minutes (now mislaid) of the meeting.
[8]   Clark, op. cit.
[9]   Council (of Senate) Minutes 285 and 322 of 12 February 1951 and 23 February 1953 in Min.I.39 and 44 respectively (University Library Archive Room). See also Neild, R (2012) *The Financial History of Cambridge University. London*: Thames River Press, pp. 54-5.

had lost sight of this precedent. The example was to be followed up by a new generation, which this time included the element missing from the CUA episode: a dedicated professional staff to support academics and powerful volunteers alike.

By this time the leadership of the university had, like Oxford, recognised the long-term threat to its international reputation through lack of funds for new initiatives, modernisation of infrastructure, and for attracting and retaining leading scholars and scientists. It was well aware of the need to develop private sources of funding. Yet university finances at Cambridge, although under pressure, were not as badly stretched as at Oxford. The academic community at large, though conscious of the long term dangers, was not ready for crisis measures.

At this time academic opinion in Cambridge was hostile to any expansion in the costs of central administration when resources for academic work were under pressure. In fact, national legislation on health and safety and work place issues, as well as growing government regulation of higher education (research assessment, teaching quality etc.) meant that non-academic costs were steadily rising. For financial, as well as for cultural, reasons, opinion had been against any expansion of 'soft' activities.

Public relations and fundraising were cases in point. The old CUA had been ahead of its time on both counts. The inaugural meeting in 1899 had adopted objectives, one of which covered communications with the wider public. It read: ' (b) To stimulate by means of meetings, communications through the press and otherwise, the interest of the country at large in the work and progress of the University as an institution of national importance',[10]. This definition of the aims of public relations has a contemporary ring, but the post war generation of academics at Cambridge, unlike Oxford, had been resistant to the idea that the university needed to explain to a wider public, including its own alumni, the value of the work it was doing and the resources needed to maintain its research and teaching to international standards. It had therefore avoided committing resources to non-academic activities like PR. So for some time the ad hoc approach was favoured. The idea of a permanent PR post was considered

---

[10]   Clark, op. cit.

on a number of occasions, usually prompted by a crisis e.g. student sit-ins in 1968 or the proposed abolition of the Veterinary School in 1989. As early as the 1960s there was a formal proposal to create a new post of University Information Officer. The financial board said there was no money. The general board (academic matters) thought the post was not necessary; and the Council of Senate noted that it hadn't been done before. In June 1972 the university had another try; it appointed a committee to consider the need for an information officer, consulting Oxford and other universities who had taken the plunge. This duly reported in November 1972 without result. On a later occasion when the matter was raised yet again, the then vice-chancellor, a distinguished scholar, opined, 'What on earth do we want an information officer for? It is only to get peoples' names in the paper.'

However, it was eventually recognised that a policy of not talking to the press was impractical. The result of the ad hoc approach was that relations with the press were conducted by a variety of academics and administrators in an uncoordinated and largely reactive way. It was not until the early 1980s in Cambridge that a more coordinated approach was developed, with the vice-chancellor's executive assistant adding the role of (unofficial) university spokesman to his other duties. The post of information officer having been formally proposed and rejected at an earlier stage, an 'information research officer' was finally appointed in 1992.[11] The university telephone directory for 2008 lists thirty-four staff members in the Office of External Affairs and Communications which perhaps suggests a tilt to the other extreme.

In this instance academic attitudes in Cambridge reflected a certain complacency, that 'good wine needs no bush', and that the merits of the university were so well known that they did not need such mundane support as a press officer and a communications policy. But the academic culture was changing.

Meanwhile the university sought to keep a low profile internally for its fundraising activities, at least until performance matched the rhetoric of fundraising targets. The Council feared that some academics would see the

---

[11]   The author is indebted to a conversation on 9 November 2011 with Geoffrey Skelsey, of the Vice-Chancellor's office, for this account.

establishment of a professional fundraising operation as diversion of resources from academic activities. There was also concern lest opinion in the colleges should turn against fundraising by the university, seeing it as a threat to college fundraising, even though no college as yet had a fundraising team. Its report therefore required the first development director to ' investigate the possibility of cooperation with the colleges though without in any way competing with college fundraising activities'.[12]

Sticking to the low profile, rather than have a development office, Cambridge decided to have a 'development unit'. In the nomenclature of the day a unit was definitely a lower form of life than a 'centre' or indeed an office. The Council was moreover at pains to emphasise that this was not a new initiative (although it patently was) but a growth of an existing (but vestigial) activity. The first duty of the new unit was to advise and assist with (existing) specific appeals. Though the director of the unit was to take the initiative in finding new sources of funds, and to undertake new fundraising projects, 'fundraising policy' was to be set by 'the Long Term Planning Committee, by the General Board and the central bodies', a bureaucratic recipe for total inertia. Fortunately in the event these bodies were too busy with their own responsibilities to oversee fundraising operations, for which there was, in any case, a separate advisory committee and a board of trustees. These many assurances that the new unit would be thoroughly supervised and regulated achieved their purpose when the Council's report to the university attracted no comments and was therefore approved without a dissentient voice.[13]

The way was thus clear for the appointment of the first director of the new unit, which was described in the job advertisement as: 'a new office, reflecting the university's intention to expand its fundraising activities and to develop new strategies to increase its income from sources other than public funds'.[14]

The university's existing fundraising activities consisted of a number of appeals initiated by departments or individuals approved by the Committee on

---

[12] 'Report of the Council of Senate on the establishment of a University Development Unit', *The Reporter*, 18 February 1987.
[13] *The Reporter*, 20 March 1987.
[14] *The Reporter*, 29 April 1987.

Alternative Funding Appeals for University Purposes. In the mid eighties there were over thirty such appeals listed,[15] which flourished or not (mostly not) based on the time individual academics could give. There were no professional staff and no central support. One exception was the Veterinary School which had established a small professional team to fundraise for an animal cancer unit and which was given further impetus over a governmental proposal, later dropped, to close the School. With these various provisos and restrictions on the freedom of operation of the new director, the search for a suitable candidate was begun.

My connection with Cambridge fundraising started with a surprise telephone call to the British Embassy in Tel Aviv one morning in the spring of 1987. Dame Anne Warburton, a former colleague of mine in the British Diplomatic Service, and at the time president of Lucy Cavendish College, Cambridge, asked to speak to me. She explained that the university wanted to start up a major fundraising operation and was seeking someone to build up the proposed operation from scratch. I was not enthusiastic. Serving in British embassies I had seen a good many fundraising events, since embassies often cooperated with good causes to provide a venue. Sensing my hesitation, Dame Anne explained the field of candidates was not very strong so I would stand a good chance. With this backhanded compliment, I said I would reflect and let her know.

The more I reflected the more I thought what an important initiative this was. From my own experience abroad I was aware of the high reputation British universities had overseas. To play a part in maintaining the quality of a leading British university seemed a worthwhile occupation. It so happened that I would be on leave at the time of the interview board, so, after due reflection, I told Dame Anne I should like my name to go forward. I was told later that at the interview 'four of the five candidates ticked all the boxes as professional fundraisers. One did not. We selected him.'[16]

The university was looking for more than a fundraiser: it also needed someone who could pilot the policy through the various internal factions and constituencies. I had thought Middle East politics complicated but academic

---

[15]   Letter dated 3 June 1985 from the University Registrary to the General Board.

[16]   Conversation of the author with James Wright, former Secretary General of the Faculties, 20 November 2011 (later vice-chancellor, University of Newcastle).

politics was something else again. I was to complete my assignment in Tel Aviv in May 1988, so it was agreed with the university authorities that I would take up my new appointment in Cambridge at the end of May 1988. While in Cambridge, I took the opportunity to call on some leading academics to get a sense from them whether they saw the new fundraising policy as a real opportunity or a waste of time and resources. I also wanted their advice on difficulties, real or imagined, academics might see, and how such objections might be dealt with. I was met almost universally with friendliness and frankness. All were agreed on the need for more funds; nearly all had constructive ideas on how extra resources could improve their work. They were invariably willing in principle to give some time to dealing with potential benefactors. Several had had bad experiences trying to organise one or other of the thirty plus (mostly abortive) university appeals with no professional help and little or no result, and were disillusioned about the prospects for success. In general they were sceptical about whether the new development unit would be able to mobilise the necessary team effort to produce results, but nevertheless willing to help when the time came.

They also summarised for me the various objections to a professional fundraising programme which they had heard from colleagues in departments or the colleges.

Cultural: Don't like talking about money
              Scared of having to ask for money
              Don't like 'fundraisers'
              Don't want 'outsiders' involved in our affairs

Academic: Dangers of loss of control
              Threat to academic independence from interfering donors
              Donors give money for what they want, not what we need
              Wrong to commit resources to fundraising which could be
              spent on academic needs

Practical: It won't work here
              We're not rich like America
              Haven't got time to help

Colleges: Don't forget they are our alumni

There were good answers to all these points, but they would come up again and again in Cambridge, and indeed in all the other universities where I subsequently worked. Nevertheless the academic consensus was moving in what was, for the work of the development unit, the right direction.

A fundraising policy

I was already convinced from my experience abroad that what attracted overseas interest in British universities was the quality and the commitment of individual scholars and scientists. I was clear therefore that academics and the university's academic plans had to lead the fundraising effort, and not the other way round. Long term plans were anyway essential if major potential donors were to be persuaded to support the university; such people would not commit time unless convinced of the importance of the university's plans, and that such plans represented the university's considered view of its long term needs.

Next was the vital need for a small group of influential individual volunteers from other walks of life who were convinced of the strength of the university's case for support, and who would give some time to help. They could provide powerful third party endorsement of the university's plans and help approaches to prospective key donors. The third element was a professional staff to generate ideas, do the preparatory work, organise events and run the back office, so that the time of academics and volunteers alike could be used to best advantage. This concept of a troika – academic/volunteer/professional – guided the thinking in preparing fundraising plans.

Before the end of my leave, I therefore wrote a paper[17] suggesting the university should elicit fresh departmental thinking, free of immediate financial and staffing constraints, on what infrastructure or other projects were needed in the long term to maintain the university's work at the highest international standards. My hope was this material could be collected and priorities

---

[17]   Internal minute to the Registary from the Development Director designate, dated 14 August 1987.

established by the university so that on taking up my appointment in May 1988, I could get to work on preparing the presentation of the university's case for support and its long term development plans to a selected group of potential donors. In the event it all took a little longer.

I spent the rest of my leave making contact with a few other universities who had development offices and were equally at the beginning of a fundraising policy and were still in the start-up phase. I also had an introduction to Warren Heeman, then vice-president for communications (PR) and development at the Georgia Institute of Technology in Atlanta, who was finishing a year at Imperial College, London on a Fulbright scholarship.

On my return to Israel, I found time to visit the fundraising departments of some universities to see some highly professional operations at work. On one such visit, the development director, a former general in the Israeli army, emphasised the need to cultivate donors before and after the gift and to keep them informed of how the gift was being used. Noting my preoccupation with winning support from academics, he reminded me that the key relationship was with the benefactors: 'It's their money.' This important point – that donors have the power of decision on how and whether to give money – was often under-emphasised or even overlooked altogether by some university departments and colleges in Cambridge during subsequent discussion over how to maximise the fundraising potential of the university community.

Later in the year in November 1987 I was sent by HMG to Atlanta, Georgia, to represent the UK at a conference on the Middle East at the Carter Centre, Emory University, organised by President Jimmy Carter. I had a free Sunday before the conference started and spent the day with Warren Heeman, who unselfishly gave me an intensive course in the elements of fundraising and the organisation of a major fundraising campaign. This confirmed my own thinking and added much practical detail when I finally started work in Cambridge in May 1988.

Before leaving Israel I went to call on an old friend, Wellesley Aron, a Cambridge alumnus who had served in the British Army during WWII, settled in Israel after the war and was then living in an experimental settlement of Jewish and Arab Israeli families of which he was a founder. I had gone to see the work of the settlement on a farewell visit, but Wellesley asked what I was going to do after leaving the diplomatic service. I told him about the new fundraising job at his old university and spoke in glowing terms of the future of the university; 'the cloud capp'd towers, the gorgeous palaces, the solemn temples' of the new academe that would be built. He cut me short, saying, 'All very good, dear boy, but don't forget the Jesus Boat Club.' This was a salutary reminder that I was going back to a collegiate university, and that the colleges and university flourished or fell together.

I fully accepted the university's policy of downplaying the implications of the new fundraising policy by having the new team keep a low profile and allotting it only a modest initial budget. I had no wish to stir up opposition before we had got started, and knew that our standing would depend on results. I also accepted, rightly as it turned out, the assurances I was given by the Registrary (the senior university administrator), Dr Stephen Fleet, that as needs arose, the necessary resources would be found. Stephen Fleet, a crystallographer, had been bursar of Downing College (and was later its master) and was uniquely trusted even by those academics who despised the Old Schools (the administrative centre) and all its works.

Nevertheless, the initial start-up was spartan indeed, and the university authorities certainly succeeded in keeping the new operation unobtrusive. Permanent offices not being ready, the development unit was housed on Trumpington Street in the University Dental Unit (another 'unit' – I was beginning to dislike the term), handy for the sub post office next door and Martin's Coffee Shop the other side, but unlikely to impinge on the consciousness of the average member of the university, student or academic. I had two staff and three chairs. We also had a telephone. But planning to be dealing with contacts around the country and internationally, and believing in the need for speed in communications (the exemplary Foreign Office communications system was my yardstick), I asked for a telex terminal to be installed. This was before the days of email and the internet. I was told there was a telex terminal already in the Scientific Periodicals Library in Bene't Street near the Guildhall (twenty minutes walk away) and I was welcome to use that. Meanwhile my request would be put to the next meeting of the relevant committee. 'When is that, next week?' I asked. 'No, next term.' Within a few weeks we were in our proper accommodation and I bought a fax machine and telex without troubling 'the relevant committee'.

The administrative arrangements likewise showed minimum public commitment. The budget was modest - £50,000 p.a. for five years; the director's performance was to be reviewed after two years and the unit after three years. Thus could any critical academic be reassured that the whole operation could be swiftly closed down if it didn't work out.

In advance of my arrival, I had negotiated for the appointment of a database officer, since one of the first tasks would be to create a database of alumni and ultimately of donors and potential donors. So long as the University of Cambridge was represented in Parliament, it had had to maintain a record of current addresses of all its graduates so they could vote in parliamentary elections for the two seats allocated to the university. With the abolition of the university seats in 1948, the university had ceased to maintain current address records of its alumni and had destroyed its old records. So the sole source of this basic information was the colleges.

Fortunately one of the members of the advisory committee overseeing the development unit was the senior bursar of St John's, Dr C.M.P. Johnson. He was a wholehearted supporter of the fundraising initiative, and explained the position to his colleagues on the bursars' committee. The support of a number of colleges, notably Trinity and King's, was immediately forthcoming, and over the next two years we secured the cooperation of every college except one, so that work of entering details of some 150,000 alumni addresses proceeded steadily. It probably helped at the working level that the database officer in question, responsible for liaising with the colleges, was Dr Alison Binns, who had been an undergraduate at King's and had a PhD in Theology – so as unlike the traditional stereotype of a fundraiser as possible.

In parallel with this routine but essential task, the academic authorities were beginning to assemble ideas and projects from department heads for the long term development plan which was needed to present a case for support to potential donors. James Wright, as Secretary General of Faculties (the senior academic administrator in the university), and I called on a variety of heads of department and other leading academics to explain why this was an essential element in preparing for a fundraising campaign, and not just another bureaucratic request which would waste more of their valuable time.

I also made a point of calling on the head of every college in the university (locally known as ' heads of house ') . Some were surprised at my request to call on them. Several had never heard of the new development unit (a success for the low profile policy?), all were receptive and hospitable. I wanted both to register the fact of the existence of this new fundraising team and to reassure them that (mindful of the Jesus Boat Club) college interests would also be taken into account. Although as yet we were far from being in a position to solicit alumni for donations, I assured each head of house that we would always include a college option in our fundraising material. It is worth noting that at this stage no college had a development office. Although most, if not all, colleges received gifts and benefactions (often in the form of legacies) fundraising was informal and ad hoc, normally carried out by the head of house or the bursar talking to old members when some particular college project was planned.

With the academic input underway, the time was now ripe for the other key element of the fundraising strategy – the recruitment of some powerful outsiders who by dint of their standing in other walks of life, could give, if convinced of the justice of the cause, third party endorsement to the university's plans, as well as setting an example as benefactors.

The Cambridge Foundation

I argued in favour of a separate foundation, independent in form, but integrated with the university and with distinguished trustees from within and without the university, and with an outside chairman. This set up would help to break down academic mistrust of 'outside interference' and enable the academic trustees to reassure their academic colleagues that the lay trustees were not barbarians seeking to tell the university what to do, but loyal, if candid, friends, ready to use their influence to support the university's plans.

Whilst the question of the Cambridge Foundation was under discussion, the then Vice-Chancellor, Michael McCrum, Master of Corpus Christi College, had already approached an alumnus whom he hoped would chair whatever form the group of outside volunteers might take. Sir Alastair Pilkington[18] was chairman of Pilkington Glass, inventor of the float glass industrial process licensed all over the world, a Fellow of the Royal Society and an honorary Fellow of Trinity, his old college.

Although somewhat concerned at the inexperience of the development director and his small staff and the exiguous budget supporting the new policy, Sir Alastair wholeheartedly embraced the concept of seeking private support to enable the university to maintain the quality of its contribution to higher education at international standards. He also readily accepted the 'low profile' approach, maintaining we should work privately in the initial phase and go public only when we had something to show for our work.

As a next step I suggested that Michael McCrum invite a small group of Cambridge alumni to a private briefing about the university's plans and to introduce the new chairman. It would also be an opportunity to seek their input and to sound out those who might be willing to give some time to the cause as well as financial support. In the early autumn of 1988, Geoffrey Howe (Trinity Hall), then Foreign Secretary in Mrs Thatcher's government, duly agreed to chair this private meeting and underline the importance to Britain's position in the world of maintaining a strong university sector working to international standards and attractive to overseas students, and to commend the efforts of Cambridge and other British universities to supplement their income from private sources.

There was a useful discussion afterwards when the vice-chancellor (and his successor to be, Professor David Williams) was able to talk informally with those present. It was agreed that as follow up I would make individual calls on all who were willing to consider supporting the university. The meeting was informal and private with some two dozen participants. For convenience it was held in London at the Oxford and Cambridge Club in Pall Mall (five minutes' walk from the Foreign Secretary's official residence). The room was not ideal since,

_____

[18]   Sir Alastair Pilkington was not a member of the Pilkington family which had founded the company. But he commented later, 'If my name had not been Pilkington, I would not have got away with breaking as much as glass as I did in developing the new product.'

to preserve the informality of the occasion drinks were served before the meeting, and there was only a scattering of chairs and armchairs such that one or two people (including me) were obliged to remain standing through the meeting.

Of course not everyone was convinced by the idea of organised university fundraising and of establishing the Cambridge Foundation to support it. I called on one of the guests who was managing director of a daily newspaper. He began by taking me to task for mismanaging the meeting (he was one of those who had had to stand). He went on to say that he would never support Cambridge because of the way his college had treated him. When he had been knighted he had been invited by the Master to dine in college as his guest. He had been flattered that his college had noticed his success in the world, and, for the first time, had bothered to pay him some personal attention. He had been seated at the right of the Master, who at one point during the meal leant over and observed that, as a successful man in his field, would he consider making a substantial donation to the college. This insensitivity to what the guest had thought was disinterested hospitality in his honour so offended him that he made his excuses and left. This was one potential benefactor (he was a millionaire) lost to the collegiate university. The episode taught me an important lesson that, for many alumni, university and college stood or fell together.

Following the Geoffrey Howe meeting, Michael McCrum, in agreement with Sir Alastair Pilkington, wrote to a number of distinguished alumni inviting them to serve as trustees of the Cambridge Foundation. Michael had served in the Royal Navy during the war and, as a former headmaster of Eton, was well connected and well versed in the ways of the world outside the ivory towers of Cambridge. He had a good feel for who, among the great and good, would be ready to help rather than just lend their name. Since a half-hearted embrace of a fundraising policy would not have attracted leading personalities to serve as trustees, the university made clear that in future 'fundraising was to be seen as an ongoing process, becoming part of the university operating practice for the foreseeable future'[19]

The university formally established the Cambridge Foundation by trust deed

---

[19] *The Reporter*, 2 November 1988, p116.

dated 12 June 1989 'to seek or provide voluntary funds for the support of education, learning and research in the University of Cambridge'.[20] The trustees were drawn half and half from inside and outside the university.[21] Those from outside included the heads of some major industrial companies, other businessmen and bankers, those from within the university being balanced between the humanities and the sciences (see Appendix G). The Royal Society, the British Academy and the CBI were also invited to nominate a trustee. The chairman had made clear from the outset that trustees were serving in an individual and personal capacity, not as representatives of their company, department or college.

At its first meeting the trustees unanimously agreed to approach the Duke of Edinburgh, as Chancellor of the University, to become Patron of the Foundation. I was anxious for this to happen as it was essential that Cambridge fundraising should be seen in the world outside Cambridge to have the backing of the highest in the land. In fact Prince Philip was more experienced than most in all aspects of charitable work. He readily agreed to become patron and always strongly supported the university's fundraising policy. He indicated informally that he would be willing to host and speak at a private reception in Buckingham Palace for potential benefactors later in the year and a date in November 1989 was appointed.

This was ideal since it provided a deadline to collect and simplify the university's long term plans for presentation to a lay audience. The private nature of the occasion was also fitting since in terms of funds raised we had little to report. Being still engaged in basic research on wealthy alumni and compiling the database, there had been scant opportunity to reconnect prospective donors with the university and to create relationships in which it might be appropriate to ask for a gift.

At this time vice-chancellors of Cambridge were drawn from among the heads of Cambridge colleges and served a two-year term. David Williams, Rouse Ball Professor of English Law and President of Wolfson College, took over as vice-chancellor in October 1989. Shortly thereafter, Prince Philip as chancellor of

---

[20]   The Cambridge Foundation: (First) Annual Report of the Trustees 1989-90.

[21]   A list of those who served as trustees in the early years (1989-95) is in Appendix E.

the university, expressed a wish to know how the university's fundraising plans were progressing and to be briefed on what the university had in mind for the presentation at Buckingham Palace in November.

There had been some discussion about what a suitable target for the campaign should be. Oxford had announced a target of £220 million but included in this total were research grants and contracts. Cambridge favoured counting only philanthropic gifts, whilst including corporate support other than contracts. The chancellor said it was essential that the university address the common perception that it was wealthy. Plainly some colleges were, but the university's future plans far outran its means. Nevertheless it had to show it was fully mobilising its own resources. If the university was not backing its own plans, why would anyone else? Likewise the financial target had to be such as to convince potential donors that a successful outcome would make a real difference to the scale and quality of its teaching and research. This was the origin of what was then, Oxford aside, the largest fundraising target of any UK university, £250 million, of which £50 million was to come from the university and colleges.

The college dimension

In addition to the many university departments, libraries, museums, laboratories and the central administration whose needs helped to account for these totals, there were the needs of the thirty-one colleges in Cambridge. A college has been defined as an 'endowed, self-governing community of scholars'[22]. The college buildings provide at least a dining hall, residential accommodation for its students, a library, and in many cases a chapel. Colleges vary greatly in wealth and thus in the extra facilities they can provide for their students such as bursaries, travel and book grants, sporting and other clubs and facilities. Anyone studying for a Cambridge degree, undergraduate or graduate, has to have a college affiliation.

In defining 'new strategies to increase its income from sources other than public funds', the university enjoined those responsible to cooperate with the colleges

---

[22]   Leedham-Greene, E. (1996) *A Concise History of the University of Cambridge.* Cambridge: Cambridge University Press, p. 243.

'without in anyway competing with college fundraising activities'. Given the importance of the alumni constituency in university fundraising, these terms of reference on the face of it raised serious problems of coordination in approaching donors. If philanthropists and major charitable foundations received multiple approaches from colleges and departments in the same university, they would rightly question whether the leadership had thought through its objectives and had settled its key priorities. The issue was not so much the tactical matter of how to coordinate bids from competing parts of the university community, but the substantive question of how best to create a positive relationship with a donor. Cambridge, like other universities, is a highly competitive place, and a change of culture was needed to take account of the needs and interest of a potential benefactor.

This was not a matter that could be settled simply by some centrally imposed decision. It required trust rather than regulation (though some agreed rules would be needed as fundraising became more complex) and a recognition of the need to present to a potential donor a successful and united institution able and ready to play a positive and growing role nationally and internationally.

The outside trustees of the Cambridge Foundation, and later the volunteers who helped the university with its major fundraising campaigns, brought just such a perspective. They were invariably keen old members of their college, yet well aware of the importance of a great university in the national economy and the wider world. They were, and are, a necessary corrective to those who took a narrower view in defending sectional departmental or college interests.

In fact there was a natural division of labour between college and university fundraising in that, in addition to shared responsibility for teaching, college needs revolve around students – their accommodation, social and sporting facilities, hardship funds and other financial needs – whilst the university's needs relate to the modernisation and expansion of libraries, laboratories, new posts for teaching and research and other facilities and research tools needed by the sciences and humanities alike.

Moreover there was one negative stereotype current in public perceptions of Cambridge which affected the entire university community: namely that it was wealthy. As mentioned above, a few colleges are indeed wealthy, but several are poor, and most just manage to pay their way. International comparison of the university community's combined endowments showed how small they were in relation to some of the great universities of North America. Their endowments for the fiscal year 2012 were:

	$US bn	[£bn][23]	League table order
Harvard[24]	30.4	[18]	1
Yale	19.3	[11.8]	2
University of Texas System	18.3	[11.2]	3
University of British Columbia	1.0	[620 million]	70

Comparable figures[25] for the top three UK universities in 2011 were:

	£bn
Cambridge	4.3
Oxford	3.9
Edinburgh	236 million

In the North American list Cambridge would have been 20th, Oxford 22nd and Edinburgh 241st. Given that the top UK universities aim to work to the best international standards, there is clearly some way to go in providing the necessary financial underpinning.

From the earliest days of the new fundraising programme it was essential to show that Cambridge was mobilising its own resources in support of its plans for modernisation, as well as seeking outside support. An early example was the Granta backbone network, a multimillion pound project which, using thirty kms of ducting and fifty-six kms of fibre-optic cabling provided data and voice services linking the eighty university and college local site networks. This was

---

[23] Approximate sterling equivalent at £1 = $1.613.

[24] National Association of College and University Business Officers (NACUBO). *NACUBO-Common Fund Study of Endowment 2012*. [online] http://www.nacubo.org/

[25] http://en.wikipedia.org/wiki/List_of_UK_universities_by_endowment.

financed jointly by the university (49 per cent), the colleges (39 per cent), the Cambridge Foundation (10 per cent) and other related users (2 per cent).

From the narrow perspective of fundraising no college in the 1980s had yet taken the plunge by investing, as the university was doing, in fundraising staff. Cambridge colleges were well behind their Oxford colleagues in this respect. Feeling that the university as a whole risked missing an important source of funds, I sounded out a number of college bursars to see if they were interested in an informal presentation on fundraising. About a dozen expressed interest including the bursar of Pembroke College, who agreed to host the event. I accordingly invited a colleague of mine, appropriately named Howard Raingold, the development director at Lincoln College, Oxford, to join in a presentation on college fundraising to college bursars. Lincoln College had developed a small and successful fundraising team. Howard therefore was able to speak from experience on the input required from a college and the returns to be expected from investment in such a new activity. He was forthright in dealing with the relationship with the university fundraising office, but nevertheless pointed out the advantages to colleges of working with the university rather than in competition. Within a couple of years of this presentation Pembroke College had recruited its first development director. Today there is only a handful of colleges without a development director or an active fundraising programme.

The university development office helped relations with colleges by offering the use of its own services in such fields as telephone campaigns, mass mailings and data processing. These services were of special interest to the poorer colleges. All however could benefit by piggybacking on major university events at home and overseas organised by the university development office which college representatives could attend or to which college benefactors or potential benefactors could be invited.

Although mutual trust and confidence between leadership groups in the university and colleges go a long way in presenting a united front to the outside world, there are inevitably problems at lower levels where individuals are less aware of the wider issues faced by the university community. The rewards and indeed the very jobs of fundraising professionals in colleges depend on their individual fundraising performance. After all, 'if the cat doesn't catch mice...'. There are bound therefore to be tensions when both university and college consider they have a link with a potential benefactor. In the United States there are sophisticated systems for the 'allocation' of such potential donors to particular fundraisers and provision for reallocation if no progress has been made within a given period. Such a system is easier (but not that easy) to operate where there is a centralised system. In a collegiate university arrangements are messier, usually based on a memorandum of understanding between university and college on how such issues are handled.

The situation is more complicated still when overseas benefactors are under consideration. There is constant pressure, understandably, from colleges with a strong fundraising team for a share in the time of Cambridge development staff based in the United States. This sometimes amounts to a bid for a share in the operational control of overseas staff. This is a dangerous area, since there has to be a single locus for decisions on the deployment of development of staff, where an overview of the university community's fundraising efforts is available, and through which a single code of ethical standards is applied. This cannot be left to individual departments (or colleges) as Lord Woolf's report on the London School of Economics made clear (see chapter 8 above). However differentiated Cambridge colleges may feel between themselves and from the university, the Cambridge name is a most powerful brand; to the outside world the fundraising activities of colleges are seen as manifestations of the University of Cambridge. After all, everyone has heard of the Cambridge spies. Few can name the colleges they belonged to.

In the early days the Cambridge Foundation was the means by which many of these tensions were resolved. With the growth of college fundraising there are bound to be strong personalities at the professional level who will push for greater influence. Best results come from strong leadership and policy direction from the university in consultation with colleges, and with the university development director as a central point for an overview of fundraising activities worldwide. The general realisation that the colleges cannot flourish without a successful university, and the university cannot flourish without successful colleges helped Cambridge to get off to a good start.

Reconnecting with the alumni

The Cambridge Foundation trustees from outside played an important role in reminding their fellow trustees from within the university that there was no real conflict between college and university interests. In the final resort the decision on where to give money rested with the donor, whatever this or that college/university fundraiser thought.

Nevertheless, the tensions and competition were there at the lower professional level; and nowhere more importantly than in dealing with the alumni. Trustees were in no doubt that the university should approach the alumni body as a whole, since unless its plans were supported by its alumni, it could hardly seek support from others. It was axiomatic that any university approach for support would include a college option, particularly since at this time no college had a development office. Since most alumni had no connection with the university (as distinct from their college) since graduation, the first issue was how to reconnect with the alumni with the university. Adrian Cadbury accordingly agreed to chair an alumni committee and Martin Sorrell chaired a marketing committee.

Trustees were clear that to raise money those approached had first to be properly informed and a convincing case made for the university's plans. Although colleges kept in touch with their own members through an annual report on college activities and personalities, the university had no contact once a member of the university had left and indeed, as we have seen, had no record of the address of their graduates. Both the alumni and marketing committees were clear that regular communication with all alumni about the university's plans and activities was essential; and that there should therefore be a regular alumni publication sent to all old members of the university. There was initially some dissent: some argued that alumni were not particularly interested in university news. They received annual college reports, and some faculties sent out a departmental newsletter – surely this sufficed?

However, the *raison d'être* of the Cambridge Foundation was the need to find substantial additional resources to maintain the quality of the university's work at international standards; and to seek therefore voluntary financing to complement the public sector support. It was absurd to argue that the university's case was not important and need not be communicated to its most important constituency.

There were arguments too about whether the university could afford the costs. Also about the frequency of communication: occasionally? Annually? Two or three times a year? Martin Sorrell (now Sir Martin), as CEO of WPP plc, a worldwide marketing services company, was in no doubt of the need to market the university's case in this way. He arrived at the crucial trustees' meeting with a score of publications which he dumped on the table. 'I'm a graduate of the Harvard Business School. These are the communications I have received from them in the last twelve months.' This ended the argument; the Foundation voted £100,000 to finance an initial publication to go to all alumni free of charge. If it proved popular, it would be continued. The first edition appeared in the autumn of 1990; and regular publication of *CAM* (Cambridge Alumni Magazine) continues to this day.

There was a separate issue which the marketing committee did not feel it was necessary to raise – namely the distribution of the publication. The development office wanted to apply the Cherokee principle[26] to the definition of 'alumnus/a' in order to reach the widest possible audience, and wished to avoid administrative arguments whether this or that course qualified a person to be considered an alumnus (as distinct from a 'graduate'). The development office also argued that a number of people who had left without a degree had nevertheless subsequently been successful in life. The alumni committee agreed and the magazine went to anyone with a Cambridge connection. Without this kind of support from the trustees such decisions, even if they came right in the end, would have taken much longer to agree through the university committee structure.

Outside trustees of the Cambridge Foundation were quite clear that the university had a duty to reconnect with its old members. The aim should be to make them feel they were part of the university for life and not just for the period they were in Cambridge studying for a degree. In developing plans to reconnect with alumni there were two hazards to be negotiated. The first concerned the colleges, who tended to look askance at any approach to 'their' old members which did not go through the college in case it weakened links with their college. The other concerned the Cambridge Society, set up in 1976

---

[26]   The Cherokee tribe apparently considered anyone with 1/64 Cherokee blood a member of the tribe.

by the then Vice-Chancellor Sir Jack Linnett, with the approval of the university, but independent of it, 'to enable past and present members of the university to remain in touch with the university and with each other'.[27] In developing university alumni activities, Sir Adrian Cadbury was well placed to finesse these hazards. He was an honorary fellow of his college (King's), an old rowing Blue, and a director of the Bank of England with impeccable business credentials as a successful director, then chairman, of Cadbury Schweppes. His personal standing reassured colleges that their interests would not suffer.

The Cambridge Society was a membership organisation based on an annual subscription and which published a well-regarded magazine. The difficulty was that it had a membership of 7,000-8,000 which, though substantial by contemporary standards, was far below where the university aimed to be, since it was only 5-6 per cent of the number of addressable alumni the university needed to reach. The Society constituted an asset for the university and any new initiatives had to avoid turf wars and be clearly seen to be additional to, not a substitute for, existing activities. There were also a large number of regional groups in the UK and abroad (some of them set up independently of and pre-dating the Society itself). Relationships with the regional and international groups were unaffected by this new departure, but there were inevitably some ruffled feathers at committee level. There was thus an initial sticky period until Bill Kirkman became Secretary of the Society and editor of its magazine. A former head of the university's careers service (and before that the Africa correspondent of *The Times*), he was fully behind the university's new policy of reaching out to the whole alumni body. With his help, Sir Adrian's commitment and the enthusiasm of the university's first alumni officer, Nicky Padfield,[28] peaceful coexistence was achieved and the new policy sailed into a bright future.

Cambridge Society events, by definition, were for its members. The alumni committee, however, wanted to develop an events programme open to all alumni. At Sir Adrian's suggestion, a pilot event was held in January 1991 among the exotic plants in the imposing sub-tropical glasshouses at the Birmingham Botanic

---

[27]   Website of the Cambridge Society.
[28]   Mrs Padfield, later a Fellow and Master of Fitzwilliam College, is a University lecturer in Law and a judge on the South Eastern Circuit.

Gardens. All alumni and their spouses in the area were invited. About sixty people attended to hear the vice-chancellor speak about the university's future plans. In parallel with organising this event, the alumni officer proposed that the university should host an alumni weekend at the end of September just before the start of Michaelmas term. Sir Adrian and the Foundation backed the idea and, to reassure the university authorities, underwrote any university costs over the approved budget of £2,000 (alumni bore their own personal expenses). Now that *CAM* was up and running there was a regular means of communication with all alumni and no extra cost was involved in publicising the event.

Again the university authorities were careful to consult widely before embarking on a precedent- creating event. In November 1990 all heads of departments and heads of colleges were written to, seeking their ideas and support for the proposal. This was followed by an open meeting for those who responded to discuss general and specific ideas for the programme. Thereafter a steering committee, headed by Dr Stephen Fleet, the senior administrator of the university, directed the planning, while a working party based in the development office was responsible for all practical arrangements. In September 1991 some 300 people attended what was generally perceived as a highly successful weekend – the first in what has become a permanent fixture.

This first alumni weekend, besides setting a precedent, was notable for four factors:

- The favourable response of the alumni to this outreach by the university (attendance subsequently grew steadily from year to year).
- The commitment and enthusiasm of individual departments and academics who gave freely of their time and precious weekends to prepare and deliver lectures and presentations.
- The substantial number of colleges which organised events to coincide with the weekend.
- The role of the external trustees of the Cambridge Foundation and their academic colleagues who backed the policy and were willing to underwrite it financially. As in the case of the alumni magazine, the speed and decisiveness of the trustees in backing a new departure helped immeasurably in securing support within the university.

One particular programme element is worth a special mention, namely the scratch choir. The university musical society (CUMS) volunteered to organise a concert with professional soloists at which alumni, on payment of a fee for the musical score, could turn up and rehearse and then perform a choral work (on the first occasion, Brahms' Requiem was chosen). Stephen Cleobury, Director of Music at King's, volunteered to conduct the first concert. The scratch choir has been a sell out every year since.

Numbers of alumni and their guests attending the weekend have grown steadily and reached a peak of over 1300 (of which over 700 were alumni) at the time of the 800th centennial year in 2009. Since then numbers have stabilised around 1000, over half of whom are alumni.

The success of the alumni weekend, restricted by definition to alumni and guests, has helped to inspire later efforts by the university to engage more broadly with the local community and the general public at large. The Festival of Science is held annually in March. Events are run by university departments and student volunteers; and in 2011 the festival attracted some 35,000 visitors over the fortnight to some 160 (mostly free) events. Building on this success, humanities, arts and social sciences run a Festival of Ideas annually in October/November. This was the first festival of its kind in the UK; again events are mostly free and in 2011 attracted some 12,000 visitors over the fortnight.

The American Friends of Cambridge University (AFCU)

Cambridge had one significant asset in the fundraising field before the 1989 decision to initiate university fundraising, namely the American Friends of Cambridge University. This had been set up by a group of American alumni in 1967 to provide a tax-efficient method for US residents to make gifts to the university. It had a board of volunteers aided by a part time accountant. AFCU made grants to college and university projects alike and was later supported at the Cambridge end by a volunteer committee and a part time administrator.[29] This

---

[29]   Initially Trevor Gardner, university treasurer 1969-83, who took on the job on his retirement. A detailed account of the early history of AFCU is in his autobiography *My First Eighty Years*, The Pentland Press, Durham 1998, Chapter XVII.

very economical operation was based on an annual mailing of up to 6,000 alumni in the US. Contributions to the collegiate university grew from US$86,000 in 1967 to US$1.26 million in 1983. During the year in which the Cambridge Foundation was established (1989) AFCU contributed over $2.1 million.

Having worked in New York and Washington for a total of seven years, I was familiar with the American approach to fundraising and well aware of the potential in terms of fundraising for higher education. I made an early point of travelling to New York to attend the AFCU board meetings. I was not entirely sure what sort of reception I could expect from the board. Would they see the development office as a threat to their position, and the development director as interfering on their patch? I had of course no such intention. The AFCU operation was efficient and well understood by colleges and university alike. The board of Trustees were eminent in their professions and gave their time voluntarily. The last thing the university wanted was to disturb a well-run organisation.

To my great relief, board members were unanimous in supporting this new and active fundraising policy. Several spoke up to say that they had long hoped for the day when the university would develop a professional operation in the US. I shared with them ideas on opening a New York office once we had decided the time was ripe to increase activity in North America. This too was heartily welcomed. The support of the AFCU board was critical in gaining the university's approval subsequently for an expansion of the fundraising effort in the US.

The AFCU board took for granted that the US operation would be fully integrated in the university's own fundraising programme, with the head of its proposed New York office reporting to the university development director. In this way they could be sure that the Cambridge case would be presented in North America as an integrated whole, without individual university departments and colleges taking uncoordinated initiatives. They, as a board, were now fully involved in the new policy since two of their members served on the board of the Cambridge Foundation, and the vice-chancellor and a college representative (at the time Dr Chris Johnson, senior bursar of St John's) served on the AFCU board, whilst the university development director attended and made regular reports to the AFCU board.

This arrangement whereby the professionals in the New York office reported to the university development director also ensured that the university at all times had an overview of Cambridge-related fundraising activities both in the UK and worldwide.

Moreover there was a further important point of policy: Cambridge was initiating a major fundraising campaign. Although the university had an international reach and fully intended the campaign to have an international dimension, it was vital to establish a firm domestic base of private financial support in the UK to which the university could refer before asking overseas donors to contribute.

The two members of the AFCU board who had been invited and agreed to serve as trustees of the Cambridge Foundation were Gaylord Donnelley (Corpus Christi), the patriarch of the Chicago printing firm (formerly president and chairman of RR Donnelley & Sons Company, the world's largest commercial printer) and Hamish Maxwell (Trinity Hall), chief executive of the Philip Morris companies. On my first visit to New York, Hamish Maxwell was in the throes of a $11.5 billion acquisition of Kraft Foods. He still found time to attend AFCU board meetings.

The personal goodwill of the AFCU board members towards the university was expressed in many ways. Hamish Maxwell was endlessly supportive and hospitable. Tom Wright (Trinity), general counsel of Princeton University, invited me to Princeton to meet their development staff. Joe Vining gave me a one-to-one tutorial on US charitable laws and the Internal Revenue Service. Gaylord Donnelley gave me hands-on help at an early stage. When on a visit to Cambridge, he invited me to accompany him on some calls on merchant banks and financial houses in the City of London. He was fitting these in on his way to Heathrow to catch his plane back to Chicago and had his suitcase with him. We took the train together from Cambridge to Liverpool Street Station. When we arrived, I offered, as the younger man, to carry his suitcase thinking we only had a short walk to the taxi rank. In fact we made three calls on City banks on foot, which meant that I arrived at each interview out of breath. I took due note of Gaylord's frugal approach to travel expenses and made a mental note to travel light on my professional calls in future.

It took another two years for the UK operations to show significant results. At that point, with the support of the AFCU board and of the Cambridge

Foundation trustees, I made the case for opening an office in New York. This meant a significant additional budgetary commitment, but Martin Sorrell came up trumps by offering vacant space in one of WPP's companies in mid-town Manhattan. AFCU board members assisted in the recruitment of the first director of the Cambridge University Development Office in the United States (CUDOUS) and a new chapter for Cambridge in America began.

Cultivation of donors

By the early 1990s university departments and colleges alike were learning the value of piggy-backing on existing university events to help build relationships between academics and potential donors. From my distorted view as a fundraiser, it was not sufficient for an event to be successful in its own terms – namely presenting some aspect of the university to a wider audience in an interesting and enjoyable way. The right people had to be there: donors who needed to be thanked, prospective donors who needed to be unobtrusively introduced to the right academic. And staff had to be there to see the event ran smoothly, to debrief the home team, and to arrange follow-up action as appropriate with prospective donors.

The Fitzwilliam Museum tour of the United States in 1989 taught us a number of useful lessons. The then director, Michael Jaffe, was totally committed to the museum and greatly extended its collections and teaching role. Keenly frustrated by lack of funds to support the work of the museum, he recognised the need to publicise the Fitzwilliam, hence his commitment to a major touring exhibition of the United States, which was sponsored by Philip Morris, thanks to Hamish Maxwell.

It was not surprising that the director saw little need to involve anyone else in the planning of this tour, despite its heavy administrative burden of logistics, insurance and security. Until the establishment of the development office, no central resource had been available to organise such a tour. The office was still new and not very well known within the university. Moreover, 'Michael Jaffe's manner and sentiments were sometimes consciously dismissive'[30] so the

---

[30]   Obituary in *The Independent*, 17 July 1997.

fledgling development office hardly registered with him as a possible source of help. Michael paid detailed attention to these arrangements and insisted that two young curators from the museum accompany the exhibits continuously, including travelling and sleeping on the long-distance lorries which transported them round the US. His determined promotion of the Fitzwilliam Museum was hampered by a failure to recognise the strength of the Cambridge 'brand' and to see the opportunity to promote the wider university at the same time without detriment to the museum's interest.

As a result, the development office was not consulted, or even informed, that the tour was taking place until after arrangements with the receiving galleries in the five venues (the National Gallery, Washington DC, the Kimbell Art Museum, Fort Worth, the National Academy of Design, New York City, the High Museum of Art, Atlanta and the Los Angeles County Museum of Art) had been made. This was unfortunate since, despite the best efforts of the part-time AFCU staff in Cambridge, they could not possibly help with, much less organise, events on the ground in five different cities, several thousand miles away. Consequently the administrative arrangements to highlight the attractions of the treasures from the Fitzwilliam Museum which rarely leave Cambridge, was left largely in the hands of the local galleries. This meant depending on the goodwill of the US hosts. Since the US galleries all had professional fundraisers on their staff, they were using the visit of these priceless pictures from Cambridge to develop events to cultivate their own donors and prospective donors. There was no mechanism for Cambridge to join in the planning, though at some venues, the Fitzwilliam was invited to suggest names for guest lists.

At one reception, there was 'no reception line, no guest list, no names, so (we) missed many potential contacts'[31]. The gala dinner in New York 'suffered from a chapter of accidents – and even perverse administration'. The date was changed at a late stage upending the plans of the dinner committee to sell 150 tickets at $1,000 dollars per head, since several pillars of New York society were unable to meet the new date. At the last minute it was disclosed that the new

---

[31]   In this account I am indebted to the diary entries for November 1989 of Stephen Bragg, administrator of the American Friends of Cambridge University, who attended the New York events.

date clashed with another major fundraising event in New York City in support of the Kimbell Museum at Fort Worth, Texas. So the date of the Fitzwilliam dinner was changed again, 'knocking out the plans of several members of the dinner committee, including the all-important Paul Mellon'. Since all these arrangements had been left in the hands of the host gallery, there was little the Cambridge side could do.

In the event a respectable turnout was achieved. Michael McCrum, the master of Corpus Christi College, who had just finished his term as vice-chancellor, was able to develop the wider Cambridge theme in his speech at the dinner and on the other public occasions. Nevertheless it was abundantly clear to the university leadership and other senior academics that, if Cambridge was to fundraise seriously in North America, it needed its own professional presence on the ground and a series of prestigious events to present the university to prospective donors – a view members of the AFCU board had held for some time.

The lessons learned from the Fitzwilliam Museum tour were taken to heart when, with the support of the chancellor, the development office organised the university's first private event for prospective supporters of the university in Buckingham Palace at the end of November 1989.

Our lack of staff meant that initially we had to tackle the few rather than the many. Thus circumstances drove us to adopt the most rewarding fundraising policy in financial terms – concentration on major potential benefactors. The Buckingham Palace reception was a good example. Drawing on experience from the Geoffrey Howe meeting and my brush with the disgruntled tycoon, I had proposed a formal sit-down presentation in the palace cinema, followed by a reception in one of the large reception rooms overlooking the gardens. Prince Philip gave his approval. At the reception there were about fifty guests, in addition to the trustees and university and college representatives. The staff made a somewhat primitive slide presentation (no PowerPoint as yet). The vice-chancellor presented the university's plans, and Sir Alastair Pilkington, as a captain of industry, spoke of the importance to the country's future of international-class universities, of which Cambridge was one. Prince Philip ended the formal proceedings with an unscripted suggestion to those present 'to go and have a look' at what Cambridge was doing. This initial introduction enabled us to begin to build relationships between potential supporters and academics which was to lead to serious support for the university's plans.

A few weeks later, I was sitting in my office and was brought a letter marked 'personal'. The envelope showed it was from a philanthropist whom I knew slightly; he had been at the palace reception and I had high hopes of a major gift. Opening the envelope I found a cheque which, at a glance, I saw had five noughts. A six-figure gift like this was indeed welcome but I had had hopes of an even larger gift. I gave the cheque to the accountant and asked him to bank it promptly. He said, 'Aren't you going to celebrate? It's the first time I've handled a cheque for a million pounds.' I had misread the number of noughts. This one transaction gave the university's fundraising policy more credibility with academics than all the exhortations in the world. It also enabled us to make a case for expanding our activities with additional staff.

Prince Philip's support was not limited to a one-off event. In January 1991 he invited the Vice-Chancellor, Sir Alastair Pilkington as chairman of the Cambridge Foundation, and myself to Sandringham, an hour and a half's drive from Cambridge, to discuss plans and stay overnight. This was a singular gesture of support as well as being an enjoyable and interesting way to brief the chancellor in the agreeable surroundings of a comfortable country house with his family around him. We arrived in time for tea, after which we had a two-hour business meeting. The chancellor said it was important to thank donors and keep in touch with them rather than ignoring them once they had made a gift. It was also important to show what use the university was making of its new resources. He offered to host an event at St James's Palace later in the year for this purpose.

This event showed that the new policy had leading academics solidly behind it. Three spoke to explain new developments: Sir Michael Atiyah, Master of Trinity, director of the new Isaac Newton Institute for Mathematical Studies, which already existed intellectually and would shortly be housed in a new building on land given by St John's and with the financial support of Trinity College; Sir Keith Peters, Regius Professor of Physic on the new worlds of molecular biology; and Christopher Greenwood, Fellow of Magdalene and a law lecturer, on the proposed new building for the Faculty of Law which had outgrown its beloved home in the centre of the university and needed still more space to deal with increasingly important developments in European and international law. Later in the year, the vice-chancellor was able to announce that the first £100 million had been raised and to thank the many donors who had made it possible. Exceptionally, The Cambridge Foundation placed a 'tombstone' advertisement in the *Financial Times*[32] to thank those donors publicly, a far cry from the days of 'we don't want our name in the newspapers'.

In between such prestigious events, the development office organised some home events to show trustees, donors and prospective benefactors and others aspects of the university's work. Up until 1991 the vice-chancellorship had been held in plurality with the headship of a college. As a result much of the vice-chancellor's official entertainment had naturally taken place in his or her college. To show as many contrasting aspects of the collegiate university's life, the development office looked for a variety of university as well as college venues for these events. Initially this did not run smoothly. In 1991, as a result of reforms in the university, the vice-chancellorship became a full-time position and could no longer be held, as had hitherto been the case, concurrently with the headship of a college. To mark this change and gently to remind people that the university had been founded before the colleges, it was decided to hold an informal presentation of academic work to the trustees and a few guests in the University Combination Room. This is part of the oldest university building, having been built following an appeal for funds by theologians in the fourteenth century. The appeal resulted in benefactions in 1369 and 1372, enabling the construction of a two-storey building, whose upper room is now the University Combination Room).[33] An appropriate venue for a meeting in support of university fundraising, one might think. The University Syndicate (committee) responsible for the University Combination Room, however, turned the idea down on the grounds that it would be too disruptive to the current users (the room was largely used by retired academics and some senior staff during the working week). Fortunately the vice-chancellor's representative on the committee ultimately was able to persuade the committee to cooperate. This handsome and venerable room proved an attractive showcase for presenting the university's work.

Other departments, when approached for help as a venue for the annual dinner of trustees and others, saw the point of hosting such an event in their department, despite (limited) disruption (they usually took place on a Saturday).

---

[32]   'The University of Cambridge thanks…' (1991). *Financial Times*, 3 December 1991, p.23.

[33]   Leedham-Green, E, op. cit., p. 25.

The development office happily tackled the task of providing a three-course meal in such surroundings as the Cavendish Laboratory, the Museum of Zoology or the newly built Sports Pavilion by the running track. College venues remain important; in their case the logistics are much simpler, being already in place. Some of the most architecturally distinguished buildings, such as the Great Hall in King's College, are regularly used for entertaining benefactors to the university and reminding guests that Cambridge is a collegiate university.

To keep in touch with donors and inspire them and other potential donors to continue to support the university's work, the university decided early in 1994 to mount an exhibition. The idea came from Sir Anthony Tennant, then chairman of Christie's and a trustee of the Cambridge Foundation, who offered Christie's premises in London's West End in January 1995 when the galleries are otherwise closed and no auctions are held. This timing was ideal, being roughly halfway through the first (ten-year) Campaign for Cambridge. The idea was to illustrate the university's past achievements and to look to the future by highlighting some leading research. The event required the enthusiastic support of university departments and colleges to be a success. Mindful of the lessons of the Fitzwilliam Museum's tour of the US, I was keen to win the maximum support within the university community for the exhibition, whilst retaining responsibility for the humdrum business of the logistics, the guest list and the calendar of events to be held in conjunction with it.

Sir David Williams, the vice-chancellor, accordingly wrote to all heads of colleges and university departments seeking their support for the exhibition and suggestions for items to be included. A committee of senior academics was set up to decide on the main themes and, with the help of an outside exhibition designer, to settle the layout in the light of items offered for display. David Williams also had the inspired idea to ask Lord St John Stevas, then Master of Emmanuel College, and a former Cabinet Minister as Minister for the Arts 1979-81 under Mrs Thatcher, to chair the Exhibition Committee. Meetings of this cross-section of scientists, philosophers and scholars took place either in the graceful board room of Grove Lodge, the residence of the Keeper of the Fitzwilliam Museum, or in the Master's Lodge at Emmanuel, where Lord St John chaired the meeting, habitually wearing purple velvet slippers embellished with the House of Lords' gold monogram. The exhibition could not include everything of special interest, and it had to strike a balance between the sciences and the humanities, the past and the present. St John Stevas's experience of interdepartmental disputes when he was in government, and his high civil service standards of chairmanship, meant that meetings rarely lasted more than an hour and moved purposefully towards decisions – a novel experience for some of the academics present.

Once the themes were clear and desirable items and artefacts to illustrate them within university and college collections were identified, it became apparent that no head of department or college would seek their governing body's approval for a loan, without cast iron guarantees on insurance and security. Again St John Stevas's experience in government came into play as he gave me an introduction to Sir Hayden Phillips, the senior civil servant in the Department of Arts and Culture (and an old boy of Cambridge County High School for Boys and an alumnus of Clare College, Cambridge). This connection resulted in a government guarantee in effect to insure the objects from the time of despatch from their owners to the exhibition until their return after their exhibition. Without this guarantee the exhibition could not have been held, since the cost of commercial insurance would have been prohibitive.

The exhibition was open to the public for three weeks during the day, and used for university and college events in the evenings. There was almost universally favourable press comment both for its content and for its purpose. Even the sub editors were kind: 'Earning as well as learning'[34]; 'Changing the world by degrees'[35]; 'Cambridge University is showing off its heritage for a good cause'.[36] Even those academics who criticised the 'clumsy boastfulness'[37] of the exhibition recognised the importance of its purpose in raising funds for higher education.

The content of the exhibition intrigued all. 'Rations taken on Captain Scott's ill fated 1911 Antarctic exhibition, fish collected by Charles Darwin on the voyage of the Beagle [...] an 8th century manuscript of the Venerable Bede, manuscripts of Tennyson's poems and Ernest Rutherford's details for splitting the atom'[38]

---

[34]   Meikle, J. (1995) *Guardian*, 3 January 1995.

[35]   Beckett, A. (1995) *The Times*, 4 January 1995.

[36]   Packer, W. (1995) 'Great Treasures from the groves of academe'. *Financial Times*, 10 January 1995.

[37]   Casey, J. (1995) 'Raising the Standard'. *Sunday Times*, 1 January 1995

[38]   *The Guardian*, op. cit., 3 January 1995.

'Here is JJ Thomson with his cathode ray tube, from the 1950s there is Crick and Watson's model of the molecular structure of DNA and from the early 19th century a fragment of Babbage's "difference engine" by which he anticipated the computer. Here is Darwin, off to the South Seas in the *Beagle* in defiance of his father's fears and admonitions that it would be uncomfortable, unsafe and a waste of time (Darwin senior's letters to his son).'[39] Other items noted by several papers included Charlemagne's personal copy of Bede dating from the eighth century, the original pamphlets of John Maynard Keynes' 'General Theory of Employment, Interest and Money', and the exquisite Canterbury Gospels from Corpus Christi College 'which date back to the 6th century when they were brought into England by St Augustine to aid his mission, and are only on public view when a new Archbishop of Canterbury is enthroned'.[40]

However successful the exhibition may have been on its own terms the point of it was to engage the alumni body and, with the help of the media, the wider public in a greater understanding of the achievements of a major British university. In this spirit, over a dozen events were held covering topics from law, engineering and management studies, a Twelfth Night Party for humanities and a Light Blue evening for sportsmen. As the chairman of the organising committee said, this was not just a heritage exhibition. It aimed to show the university at work and to convince prospective donors that its work was worth supporting.

Consolidation

By the end of Sir David William's term of office as vice-chancellor in 1996, the University of Cambridge had all three elements of the troika up and running. There was a clear long-term plan for the expansion and modernisation of teaching and research, backed up by dedicated scholars and scientists able and willing to explain their activities to potential benefactors; a committed group of powerful volunteers from outside the university to help argue the university's case and to initiate relationships with potential corporate and individual donors; and a well-equipped staff in Cambridge and New York, over forty-strong with growing professionalism and a budget of over £1 million per annum to support academics and volunteers, organise events and briefings, and perform all the usual back office

---

[39] *Financial Times*, op. cit., 10 January 1995.
[40] Gerard, L (1995) *Independent,* 6 January 1995.

functions. By the end of 1991 the university had raised £100 million from its own and from external sources towards its ten-year target of £250 million. By the year 2000 the £250 million target had been comfortably exceeded.

The start of the new millennium came halfway through Sir Alec (now Lord) Broers' vice-chancellorship (1996-2003). Lord Broers had spent twenty years in industry before returning to academia in 1984 as Professor of Electrical Engineering and subsequently Head of Department of Engineering, and Master of Churchill College. He was therefore well placed to consider future plans for developing the university's work. In providing the technology and resources necessary for both the humanities and the sciences, he made clear in his inaugural address, that 'our new sites offer tremendous potential but [...] this will only be realised through collaboration with business and industry and with extensive fundraising. It is therefore our intention to continue with the appeal initiated seven years ago.'[41]

Thus the policy of the university leadership in 1987 of proceeding little by little to install a properly resourced fundraising operation as a permanent feature of the university's activities came to fruition. Indeed, Lord Broers, recognising the opportunity presented by the 800th anniversary of the origins of the university in 1209, initiated planning for a future fundraising campaign of a different order of magnitude - with a target of £1 billion, then the largest ever of any UK university. This goal was reached under his successor, Dame Alison Richard (vice-chancellor 2003-2010) who initiated the 'silent' phase of the campaign in 2003, presided over the public launch of the campaign in 2005 and its successful conclusion in 2010. The 800th anniversary campaign reached its £1 billion milestone two years early in 2010, but the new vice-chancellor, Professor Sir Lezek Borysiewicz, confirmed that the campaign would continue as planned to 2012: 'but of course our need to fundraise will not stop there [...] Philanthropy will play a critical role in maintaining both our excellence and our ability to take the risks essential to path-breaking research, whilst sustaining our teaching.'[42]

The low profile had gone, and fundraising in Cambridge had come to stay.

---

[41] Speech given by Professor Sir Alec Broers on his installation as vice-chancellor (1996). *The Reporter* 1 October 1996.

[42] Message from the Vice-Chancellor in the Cambridge 800th Anniversary Campaign Report 2009-2010, p.4.

List of Appendices

Appendix A:
Membership of CASE/UK ad hoc committee 1989-94

C W Squire (chair)	Cambridge University
Adrian Beney	Durham University
Alison Binns	Cambridge University
Colin Boswell	Kent University
Sue Boswell	Goldsmith's College
Helen Cane	UMIST
Keith Copland	Leeds University
Bobby de Joia	Middlesex Polytechnic
Neil Dorward	PCL
Ray Footman	Edinburgh University
Kay Honner	St Hilda's College, Oxford
Barry Jackson	PCL
Jo James	Lancaster University
John Jones	University of Wales
Bob Masterton	Open University
Craig Mathieson	Luton College of Higher Education
John McLoughlin	LSE
Geoffrey Middleton	Nene College
Steve Montgomery	UCL
Dave Pallet	Reading University
Jill Pellew	Imperial College
Sue Rees	Anglia Polytechnic
Moyra Sutcliffe	Nottingham University
Janet Walters	Oxford Polytechnic
Theresa Waters	Strathclyde University
Philomena Wilson	Sheffield City Polytechnic

Note: this group met as needed from 1989 until the end of negotiations with HEERA and the establishment of a CASE (Europe) office and charitable trust in 1994.

Appendix B:

The First CASE UK Institute in Alumni Relations and Fundraising

University of Edinburgh, September 1990 : Speakers and Presenters

United Kingdom

Alison Binns	Assistant Director	University of Cambridge
Colin Boswell	Development Director	University of Kent
Helen Cane	Alumni Officer	UMIST
Keith Copland	Development Director	University of Leeds
Neil Dorward	Pro Rector	PCL
Ray Footman	Director, Info and PR	University of Edinburgh
Jo James	Development Director	Lancaster University
Bob Masterton	Secretary to the Business School	Open University
Colin McCallum	Development Director	University of Strathclyde
Iain More	Consultant	Iain More Consultants
Bill Squire	Chair of CASE Europe Task Force Development Director	University of Cambridge
Moyra Sutcliffe	Graduate Liaison Officer	University of Nottingham
John Wynn Jones	PR and Info Officer	UC North Wales, Bangor

North America

Ed Allenby	VP Advancement	College of William and Mary
Bob Behr	Director of Alumni Relations	Williams College
Ben Hancock Jr	VP for Institutional Advancement	Albion College MI
Warren Heeman	VP for Development and AR and past chair of CASE	University of Chicago
Bill McGoldrick	VP for Institute Relations	Rensselaer Polytechnic Institute
Gavin Ross	Exec Director	McGill Graduates Society, Montreal
Sue Washburn	VP for University Relations and Chair of CASE	St Lawrence University NY

Programme

CASE UK Institutes in Alumni Relations and Fundraising at the University of Edinburgh
23-26 September 1990

Institutes Programme

NOTE:

    P = Plenary session (common to Alumni Relations and Fundraising)

    A = Alumni Relations track

    F = Fundraising track

Those attending the Institutes may opt for a session outwith their own track where space permits.

Sunday 23 September

2-5.30pm	Arrival and registration at St Leonards Reception
7.30-8.15pm	(P1) **Introduction to the Institutes** by BILL SQUIRE, Chair of CASE Europe Task Force and RAY FOOTMAN, Edinburgh organiser of the Institute

                      Can it be done here?

                      - Can North American experience of advancement transfer to this side of the Atlantic?

                      WARREN HEEMAN

8.30-9.30pm	(A1) **Icebreaker session**

                      - Introduce yourself and your work to others on your track and meet the AR Institute Faculty

                      BOB BEHR, RAY FOOTMAN & AR FACULTY

                      (F1) **Icebreaker session**

                      - Likewise for Fundraising

                      - COLIN BOSWELL, BEN HANCOCK AND FR FACULTY

Monday 24 September

08.30-10am   (A2) **Mounting an AR programme**
               - aims and objectives
               BILL MCGOLDRICK, GAVIN ROSS, RAY FOOTMAN

               (F2) **An A-Z of higher education fundraising**
               - a 'soup to nuts' overview
               SUE WASHBURN, COLIN BOSWELL

10.10-10.45am Coffee and opening of the Trade Exhibition in Room 24 by
               WARREN HEEMAN

10.45-12.15pm (P2) **Starting small**
               - AR & FR programmes from a modest resource base
               BEN HANCOCK, BOB BEHR, JOHN JONES

12.30-1.30pm lunch
2-3.30pm   (A3) **Organising the AR Office and framing AR policy**
               BILL MCGOLDRICK, MOYRA SUTCLIFFE

               (F3) **The Role of Research**
               SUE WASHBURN, COLIN BOSWELL

4.15-5.45pm   (P3) **Tracing and documenting alumni and using the
               database**
               BOB BEHR, BILL MCGOLDRICK, HELEN CANE,
               ALISON BINNS

6-7pm   Dinner

8-9.30pm   (A4) **Establishing and making use of networks**
               BOB BEHR, GAVIN ROSS, NEIL DORWARD

               (F4) **Solicitation**

- Who's the target and what's the method?
BEN HANCOCK, COLIN BOSWELL

Tuesday 25 September

08.30-10am   (P4) **Communications, Liaison & Awareness**
BILL MCGOLDRICK, RAY FOOTMAN

10-10.30am   Coffee

10.30-12 noon (A5) **A home from home for alumni on campus?**
BOB BEHR, CALLUM CALDER

(F5) **Capital Campaigns and Major Gifts Programmes**
ED ALLENBY, JO JAMES

12.10pm   **Annual Giving**

2-3.30pm   (P5) **Alumni, faculty and friends as volunteers**
BILL MCGOLDRICK, GAVIN ROSS, ED ALLENBY, COLIN MCCALLUM

4-5.30pm   (A6) **Reciprocation**
- return to Alumni
BOB BEHR, GAVIN ROSS, MOYRA SUTCLIFFE

(F6) **Approaching Corporations and Trusts**
SUE WASHBURN, KEITH COPLAND, BOB MASTERTON

8.15pm   Conference dinner, Playfair Library Hall.
Main guest: Sir David Smith, Principal and Vice Chancellor of the University of Edinburgh

Appendix C:
Participation in CASE Europe annual conferences 1990-2011

Year	Venue	Delegates	Exhibitors*	Total
1990	Edinburgh	127	12	139
1991	Kent	140	n/a	
1992	Lancaster	150	n/a	
1993	Cambridge	248	n/a	
1994	Telford (Wolverhampton)	250	n/a	
1995	Nene (Northampton)	285	n/a	
1996	Durham	Separate figures not available		425
1997	Brunel Uxbridge	Separate figures not available		450
1998	Queens University, Belfast	Separate figures not available		453
1999	Westminster University, London	350	62	412
2000	Warwick	380	94	474
2001	Heriot Watt	442	67	509
2002	Nottingham	428	91	519
2003	Cardiff	391	n/a	
2004	Hertfordshire	425	n/a	
2005	Heriot Watt	553	n/a	
2006	Nottingham	526	n/a	
2007	Heriot Watt	615	n/a	
2008	Hilton Metropole, Brighton	652	n/a	
2009	Conference Centre, Liverpool	600	n/a	
2010	Conference Centre, Glasgow	670	n/a	
2011	Conference Centre, Manchester	654	n/a	

Note: *CASE provided exhibitor space every year and each conference has been strongly supported by exhibitors, but separate figures are not always available.

Appendix D

a) CASE Europe training events for selected years[1]
(in addition to annual conferences)

Year	UK	Other Europe
1993	None	None
1998	?	?
2003	16	1 (Dublin)
2008	27★	3 (Dublin 2, Stockholm)
2011	46★	2 (Rome, Paris)

★Supported by HEFCE under the capacity building and matched funding programme

b) Number of staff members in London

1994	1
1998	3
2003	7
2008	10
2011	13

---

[1]   Information supplied by CASE Europe, 2 December 2011.

Appendix E:
Vice-chancellors' ad hoc group 1999-2007

Attended original meeting 29 September 1999

Professor C Duncan Rice	Principal and Vice-Chancellor University of Aberdeen Co-Chairman
Professor David VandeLinde	Principal and Vice-Chancellor University of Bath Co-Chairman
Professor George Bain	Vice-Chancellor The Queen's University, Belfast
Professor Sir Alec Broers	Vice-Chancellor University of Cambridge
Sir Stewart Sutherland	Principal and Vice-Chancellor University of Edinburgh
Professor John Quelch	Dean London Business School
Professor Lord Currie	Deputy Dean London Business School
Mr Roger McClure	Pro-Rector The London Institute
Professor Sir Colin Campbell	Vice-Chancellor University of Nottingham
Sir Anthony Kenny	President of the OU Development Programme University of Oxford
Professor Chris Llewellyn Smith	Provost University College London
Professor Ron Cooke	Vice-Chancellor University of York
Professor Sir Brian Follett	Vice-Chancellor University of Warwick
Also Professor Frank Rhodes	President Emeritus Cornell University (President 1977-95)

Attended one or more subsequent meetings

Birmingham University
Bristol University
Brunel University
Cardiff University
City University
Glasgow University
King's College London
Loughborough University
London School of Economics
St Andrew's University
School of Oriental and African Studies
Southampton University
Strathclyde University

Appendix F:
Participation in annual survey of gift revenue and costs

Year Covered	No. of Institutions	Sponsor
1999 – 2000	10[1]	VC ad hoc Group
2001 – 2002	17[1]	VC ad hoc Group
2002 – 2003 (thereafter annually)	24[2]	Ross Group
2010 – 2011	167[2]	Ross/Case

---

[1]   Present writer's archive
[2]   Ross–Case archive

Appendix G:
Cambridge Foundation Trustees 1989 – 1995

Professor P P G Bateson	Provost of King's College
Professor GPK Beer	President of Clare Hall
Professor R J Bowring	Professor of Modern Japanese Studies
Professor Lord A N Broers	Master of Churchill College, Vice-Chancellor 1996-2003
Sir Adrian Cadbury	Chairman, Cadbury Schweppes Director, Bank of England
Sir John Craven	Chairman, Morgan Grenfell Group plc
Professor Sir Sam Edwards	Cavendish Professor of Physics
Lord Flowers	Chairman, Nuffield Foundation
Sir David Li	Director and CEO, The Bank of East Asia Ltd
Mr T James	Chairman, Schering Holdings
Dr C M P Johnson	Fellow and Bursar, St John's College
Sir Paul Judge	Chairman, Food from Britain
Professor Lord Lewis	Warden of Robinson College
Mr M W McCrum	Master of Corpus Christi, Vice-Chancellor 1987-1989
Mr H Maxwell	Chairman of the Executive Committee, Philip Morris Companies Inc.
Sir Alastair Pilkington	Chairman, Pilkington Glass
Sir David Simon	Chairman, The British Petroleum Company plc
Sir Martin Sorrell	Chief Executive, WPP Group plc
Professor B E Supple	Director, The Leverhulme Trust
Sir Anthony Tennant	Chairman, Christie's International plc
Professor J O Thomas	Professor of Macromolecular Biochemistry
The Rt Hon Baroness Trumpington	Baroness in Waiting former Mayor of Cambridge

Professor Sir David Williams QC	President of Wolfson College, Vice-Chancellor 1989-1996

In attendance

Dr Stephen Fleet	Registrary, former Bursar of Downing College
Dr James Wright	Secretary General of the Faculties, former Bursar of St Catherine's College
Joanna Womack	University Treasurer, former Bursar of Trinity Hall
C W Squire	Secretary of the Foundation, University Development Director

Acknowledgements

I acknowledge with thanks the help of the Council for the Advancement and Support of Education (CASE) for free access to and permission to quote from the CASE archive in Washington DC. I also wish to thank John Wiley & Sons Inc for permission to draw on tables 4.1, 4.2 and 6.9 from *The Shaping of American Higher Education* (2010), by Arthur Cohen and Carrie Kisker; and the University of Virginia Press to draw on figure 3.1 in *Equity and Excellence in American Higher Education* (2005), by William Bowen, Martin Kurzweil and Eugene Tobin.

I have also had invaluable information and comment from a wide variety of individuals involved in university fundraising. My thanks are due to them all. I am particularly grateful to the following: Peter Agar, University of Cambridge; Hardip Begol, Department of Education and Skills; Mary Blair, London School of Economics; Colin Boswell, University of Kent; Stephen Bragg, University of Cambridge; Charles Clarke, Secretary of State for Education and Skills 2002-04; Christopher Cox, University of Manchester; Jackie Cox, University Library, Cambridge; Stephanie Edwards, CASE Europe; Ray Footman, University of Edinburgh; Megan Galaida, CASE HQ, Washington DC; Kate Hunter, CASE Europe; Fiona Kirk, London School of Economics; Ian Lewis, Higher Education Funding Council for England; Alisdaire Lockhart, University College London; Anne Lonsdale, University of Cambridge; Iain More, Iain More Consultants; Joanna Motion, CASE; Lord Neill, University of Oxford; Philip Nye, Department of Business, Innovation and Skills; Nicola Padfield, University of Cambridge; Gemma Peters, King's College London; Geoffrey Skelsey, University of Cambridge; Miles Stevenson, University of Sheffield; Moyra Sutcliffe, University of Nottingham; Eric Thomas, University of Bristol; Ruth Thompson, Department for Eduction; Jon Walker, University of

Loughborough; Lady (Diana) Warwick, Universities UK (UUK); Martin Williams, Department for Business, Innovation and Skills; James Wright, Universities of Cambridge and Newcastle.

Special thanks are due to John Glier of Grenzebach Glier and Associates for his financial support and much else.